A Woman's Book of Days

A Woman's Book of Days

Northstone 

Editor: Michael Schwartzentruber
Cover design: Lois Huey-Heck
Consulting art director: Robert MacDonald
Cover illustration from Public Domain, colored by Lois Huey-Heck

Northstone Publishing Inc. is an employee-owned company, committed to caring for the environment and all creation. Northstone recycles, reuses and composts, and encourages readers to do the same. Resources are printed on recycled paper and more environmentally friendly groundwood papers (newsprint), whenever possible. The trees used are replaced through donations to the Scoutrees For Canada Program. Ten percent of all profit is donated to charitable organizations.

Canadian Cataloguing in Publication Data
Sinclair, Donna, 1943-
A woman's book of days

Includes index.
ISBN 1-896836-02-X

1. Women—Spiritual life—Meditations. 2 Women—Conduct of life. 3. Devotional calendars. I. Title.
BL625.7S46 1997 291.4'32 C97-910154-9

Published by Northstone Publishing Inc.

Printing 10 9 8 7 6 5 4 3 2 1

Printed in Canada by
Friesen Printers
Altona, MB

Acknowledgments

I read bits of this book to five friends – we call ourselves, immodestly, The Jung Group – who gather once a month to talk. I was still reeling from the effort of writing down pretty much everything I knew. "But of course, you've been getting ready to write this all your life," said one.

It's true. And so it would be impossible to name all the authors whose work has delighted and instructed me for years, and whose thought, therefore, informs this book. But there are some who have a special place: Dorothee Soelle, Thomas Moore, James Hillman, Walter Wink, Henri Nouwen, Esther de Waal and Jean Shinoda Bolen. Polly Young-Eisendrath's *Hags and Heroes* (Inner City Books, 1984) alerted me to the Arthurian legend adapted and retold in the entry for May 25.

I'm grateful to three young women I find in my kitchen some mornings – my daughter Tracy and two of her friends, Erin Shillinglaw and Laure Lafrance. Their inquiries and their counsel led me to believe there might be readers for this book.

There is no way I can adequately thank Wanda Wallace, Kathy Aylett, Rose Tekel, Sarah Tector, Trish Mills and Muriel Duncan for their wisdom.

I am grateful to the people who have allowed me to tell their dreams.

I am, as always, thankful for the way my family – my mother, Margaret Knapp; my brother, Larry Knapp; my children, David, Andy and Tracy Sinclair; and my husband, Jim Sinclair – trust me to tell stories about them. My mother, especially, has graciously allowed me to attach her name to two of her dreams.

I'm grateful to Michael Schwartzentruber and the staff at Northstone for their patience and excellent advice.

To Jim,
whose respect for women,
and love for this one in particular,
always gives me strength.

Introduction

When I first thought of doing a book of days, I pictured meditative passages sufficient for one year. I would casually produce 365 pieces of wisdom. Willing readers would then absorb one a day like a vitamin, slipping it down with their coffee before heading off to work.

It didn't work that way. If I have any wisdom at all, it doesn't flow like water.

So I pondered how I spend my days; surely I had some inkling they contained something of value or this idea wouldn't have surfaced at all.

I have the good fortune to spend my time as I like. Reading, writing, talking with people, gardening, walking, thinking, pacing while I think, cooking dinner, throwing towels in the washing machine, reading. These are not leisurely days. They are jammed. I have no real ability to set limits about the work I take on, and I like to do it as well as I can. Writing means intense research and interviews and polishing words while hungry deadlines wait. Reading describes the leisure activity of a woman who must inhale magazines, newspapers, essays, fiction of all kinds or go mad.

This book comes out of that reading and writing. But mostly it comes from the talking. Women talk to one another. There is a peculiar energy to their conversation, an inability to hear another's pain or joy or worry without entering into it. They join stories. They try to understand what they mean. And out of the spaces between them, out of laughter wrinkled with unshed tears, comes wisdom.

I have tried to gather into these pages what I have learned from women, and men too, who have this odd gift of empathy, this soul-friendship. I hope it will give you something for each day that is more than a daily dose of meditation. I hope it will invite you into a spiritual conversation that will sift through your mind and heart for a year.

JANUARY

January 1: **Resolutions**

These are the longest nights. Sometimes I sit down at my desk these January mornings while it is still dark and by the time I finish work, it is dark again.

Oh, I get up to pace the house while a paragraph untangles in my head, to let the dog out or shovel the front steps so the mailperson can get through. But these days move fast from an orange glow on one horizon to an orange glow on the other.

But in between, this sun on snow so bright

it's hallucinatory. Perhaps that's why these days are made so short; we couldn't bear too much of this unearthly loveliness, this golden light that only visits at this time, these groaning frozen paths beneath our feet.

So I will change. I will walk in the cold each day. I am a child of winter, and I will go out and make snow angels to play with me.

New Year's resolutions help us see the possible, so we can reach toward it.

January 2: **Happiness**

It's a temptation to pursue happiness with fervor, buying things to the limit we can afford and amending our universe to the extent of our ability.

Nothing wrong with that. I have a wish list miles long. But happiness doesn't come from owning a home, planting a garden, redecorating the living room.

These all give us pleasure.

But happiness comes from inside. You turn around one day and observe its elegant presence, flitting like a dragonfly past your vision, the awareness of it gone in an iridescent instant.

Happiness is an elusive visitor. When it arrives, sit down. Talk. Perhaps, welcomed, it will stay.

January 3: **Anticipation**

The seed catalogues are coming in now. Next summer is far away. That's fine, I'm still resting from the tasks of the last one.

But the joy of being human is our ability to live in the future, to dream, plan, and perceive a vision as if it were reality. Not just of gardens, but of our lives.

January 4: **Forgiveness**

Whoever put "forgive and forget" together in the same phrase is in need of mercy themselves.

As a woman I need to learn how to forgive myself and others fully.

It's too exhausting to carry around a torch of rage that threatens to burn you to the ground. There has to be a way to pour water on it: accept the limitations of our fellow-humans, accept our own.

Forgive.

But not forget. Those charred bits of well-soaked anger need to sit on a tidy shelf in our soul. We can glance at them, occasionally, to keep from getting burned again.

Memory and grace are hidden together in every act of forgiveness.

January 5: **Mercy**

There are days you wish you could get back to do over. Once, when I was a very young high school teacher, passionate about my subject, the football coach came to me. His best quarterback had failed English. My class. According to school rules, that meant he couldn't play, and could I just find a couple of extra marks here and there.

No, I said. I was full of high standards. I can't remember if I even offered to give the football star extra help, but I hope I did. No amount of pleading would move me, I was principled.

It took years and motherhood and hanging around some wise people to teach me that the first principle is care of the child. Football was the only thing he could do well. It was keeping him in school. Mercy was called for, and I offered judgment.

I wish I had that day back again.

There is a time to judge, and a time to be merciful. Whenever we have power, we have to know which time it is.

January 6: **Reality-testing**

A good friend has pretty much raised her child – a thoughtful, wonderful teen – alone.

Sometimes, though, when she hits a bump on the road of parenting, she phones, wonders if I have time for lunch. She arrives bearing homemade soup and questions. What do I think of this situation, what would I have done? And always: Am I overreacting?

She's checking out her view of reality with a trusted friend. I am honored. And I learn from her how wise it is to test our version of "what's-going-on-here" with other people. Not only in mothering, in every crucial thing we do.

Asking for alternate views doesn't mean we have to accept them blindly; it just gets us a little closer to reality.

January 7: **Masks**

We are held back sometimes from asking for help by our own vision of who we are. For instance, I really like to help people. I like to be counselor and sage.

I fulfill these roles not badly. Sometimes I do workshops, playing expert for a whole weekend.

It's not that these roles aren't real; they are. But they are only a small part of my story. If they get too strong and I start to believe that I'm never unsure or lost, I will develop a thick crust over my soul that will never let me ask for help again. That would be the death of any energy in me that is valuable.

Authenticity isn't easy. It's just essential.

January 8: **Waking at night**

I'll go for weeks, sleeping like a baby. Suddenly one night, I'll be up at three a.m., tossing, aware of my failures, worrying about the people I love.

We are vulnerable and alert at that hour. We're probably overreacting, too, but it's not a good time to call a friend to get a bigger picture.

But this is valuable time. This is when we do our thinking, seeing things our busyness and self-sufficiency won't let us see during the day. Insomniac nights are good for writing things down, making lists, keeping a journal. The light of morning is fine for acting on what's helpful and burning the rest.

January 9: **Food**

Women's lives revolve around food. It's what we bring instinctively when we want to support someone stressed or in pain. A good friend appears at my door, cheerfully hands me a cup of takeout coffee from our favorite donut place, and vanishes when she knows I'm in trouble with a deadline.

The last time there was a family funeral, she sent over a whole roasted chicken complete with low-fat gravy. We were all too absent to eat properly, we just kept tearing off chunks as we went by, or heating up chicken sandwiches with gravy in the microwave.

She has women's wisdom. So did Jesus. He got everyone around the table, rich, poor, old, young, stressed or laughing, sharing bread, erasing differences, tending the body. He knew it was not separate from the soul, knew that all food offered in love is soul-food.

January 10: **Double-quick dinner rolls**

1 cup very warm water
1 pkg instant dry yeast
2 tbsp sugar
2 1/4 cups flour
1 tsp salt
1 egg
2 tbsp soft shortening

Mix yeast with flour and sugar and salt. Stir in shortening and water, and then eggs. Mix. Let rise. Beat down and let rise again. Spoon into 12 greased muffin cups, sprinkle with sesame seeds or poppy seeds. Let rise again (about 20 min.) and bake 15 to 20 min. at 400°F.

Fast enough to be made on impulse and taken to a friend.

January 11: **Treasure within**

Around a table, visiting. "I had the *weirdest* dream last night," someone ventures. Others listen attentively. The telling and listening is enough to honor the dream.

It's too bad some tell dreams only to a therapist. Professional care, while helpful, carries the inference of problem. But dreams are an everyday matter, not of illness, but of delight. They are filled with puns and laughter.

Friends can help ponder the questions a dream asks. For a dream of a runaway car we can say "Hmmmm," just as well as a psychiatrist. "Is part of your life out of control?"

For a dream of fabulous antiques we can say:

"What hidden treasures within yourself do you not see?"

We don't offer answers to the questions; that's for the dreamer to do. We just delight in the dream's wisdom and care. Dreams, like friends, seek our well-being.

January 12: **Celebration**

Women have always celebrated small moments. Remembering the favorite meal when a grown son or daughter comes home to visit. Gathering friends for a birthday: cake and ice cream and wicked cards. Wedding showers, baby showers. Candles and pizza on the edge of the weekend, the time of re-creation, hooray.

It is poetry in mime, these graceful gestures – the salute of wineglasses even over macaroni; the lighting of a candle just because it's suppertime and the day is almost over and we are still alive and here together. Hooray.

Or better we might call these actions murmered prayer, a continuous inaudible litany of praise for each other's lives. "May you live long and well," these gestures say. "May the blessing of your presence continue."

We honor thus the god of everyday. We remind each other of our love. Hooray.

January 13: **Grace note**

We should paint the kitchen ceiling. And the walls, but the ceiling is the worst. It's been almost a year since our 17-year-old daughter was making felafel with her buddies. The hot oil in the big black cast-iron frying pan caught fire. They tried to smother it without success, the fire extinguisher, out of sight, forgotten. Finally Tracy wrapped her hands in a towel, picked up the blazing pan and threw it out the back door.

She could have been burned. When someone opens a door holding a fire, the gust of oxygen makes it flare. Usually it blows back into their face.

"All I could think was how much Mom loves this house," she said.

Her hair was singed. When we got home, unaware, one of her friends was tearfully trimming it with the kitchen scissors. We spent the afternoon scrubbing the ceiling and walls, but oily streaks remain.

We should paint it. But every time I look at those streaks, I think how my daughter, who could have been burned, is safe.

Grace is a gift that arrives in the midst of chaos.

January 14: **Dogs**

Our dog, Gabriel, has a number of functions. He alerts us when a squirrel crosses the invisible barrier he has erected around the house. The alert does no good, of course. Gabe rushes from window to window in a noisy frenzy and the squirrel looks in amused.

He greets visitors carefully. He keeps our feet warm by lying on them. He accepts small offerings from our plates with dignity, knowing he has a right as a valued member of the household.

It is impossible to walk Gabriel, since he takes his name seriously. He is such a guardian he must be muzzled to prevent him attacking passersby in the conviction each is an axe-murderer. The fact we ungratefully choke him while he goes about this civic duty is entirely tangential.

He sheds.

He is not perfect, but he lives assured in his imperfection. He accepts himself for what he is, a runty Sheltie whose great gift is to love unconditionally.

Like him, we are not called to be perfect. We are only called to be loving.

January 15: **Differences**

My husband is an extrovert, and I am an introvert. We are, therefore, utterly incompatible. Our marriage is a miracle, held together by love and continuing astonishment at each other's alien ways.

We go for a walk, and he talks. I am quiet, thinking. He tells me the history of every house we pass. He knows these stories, because he is an extrovert, and bothers to find out. I remind him he has told me the same story twice before. He is undaunted.

He is busy greeting people, talking to strangers, luxuriating in the joy of human companionship. I am walking. That's enough for me.

We thrive as a couple because we each think this is remarkably funny, and because we do not believe different ways of being constitute ornery behavior. There's an infinite number of ways to approach the world. One way is not better than the other; it just is.

January 16: **Fire**

These short dark days need fire. I light candles and a faint warm scent of vanilla fills the air.

And I light a fire in the fireplace. We will never convert it to gas even though this is an old house and cold and the logs have to be carried in and the ashes carried out and I know it sucks all the heat out of the rest of the house.

Never mind. I need fire. I need the sound of it, the faint smoky warm smell drifting through the house, the heat on my back when I sit on the hearth to talk with a friend.

Some ancestor, still alive in me after all these

centuries, comes in flame to comfort me, to remind me of the sun of coming spring.

If we don't light fires or candles in the dark, we might forget how memory and hope, twinned, pull us through our days.

January 17: **Sacred places**

Jerusalem. Iona. Chartres. People travel to these sacred places seeking visions only possible in the radiance of God. All Creation is filled with that light; but there are certain places that throw memory and future together with such precise force that the everyday is torn away, and we can see clearly what is mostly hidden from our eyes.

Many of us find those sacred places in the natural world – mountain, forest, lake. Here we make our pilgrimages, or dream of it. While environmentalists crusade over it, theologians (some of them Native) redefine its place from that which we dominate to that which we respect. The north, the back country, the untouched grasslands, the sea enshrine for us the Grail.

Our sacred place, called up from memory, can heal us on a January day.

January 18: **Sabbath**

Sunday mornings I sleep in. I read the unfinished sections of the Saturday paper with breakfast. I enjoy the quiet streets. Often I go unhurried to church in my jeans. Surely God would rather have me here like this than not here at all.

We need these quiet days to remember that we are more than our work. There is more to life than accomplishment. We are creatures with souls, creatures who seek to understand what and who we are.

And even if we are not "religious," we are part of Creation. We are holy, therefore, and worthy of rest.

January 19: **Connections**

A memory. I am very young, three or four years old, trailing my hand over the side of a rowboat. My father is rowing; we are going on a picnic. The sun is warm, and I know I am not separate from the water or the sun or the creaking oars or my father.

I couldn't have put that into words then. It wasn't that I had no concept of connection; I had no understanding of separation. That came later, a hard learning, one I resisted but eventually accepted.

Some films now revive that memory. I am learning respect for that four-year-old's wisdom. *Nell, Phenomenon, Powder, Six Degrees of Separation*, all accept as given that we are all connected. All creatures, great and small, sharing the touch of the Creator.

January 20: **Singing**

I can't sing very well. But I belong to a church choir. I love to be part of something that is sometimes beautiful.

We make mistakes, of course. Me especially. We come in too soon or not at all, one of us fluffs a line and everyone else covers up. But this little collection of ordinary people, some talented, some not so, all do our best to make the others sound good.

That's what makes us a community. We forget ourselves in the music and the shared joy in praising Creation, being – in our care for one another – both the singer and the song.

Treating others and ourselves with equal love is a kind of singing.

January 21: **Wisdom**

Wisdom is generally the province of the old or very young. Small children offer wisdom because their very innocence gives them questions to point the way out of some dilemma.

The old have wisdom because they have made so many mistakes.

Those who don't risk enough to make mistakes may be safe, but never wise.

January 22: **Friends**

We set up wild schedules, to keep away the midwinter dark.

There may be good friends we see too little, especially if we are phone-phobic or introverted. We may not notice that the minimum requirements of friendship – shared laughter, tears, a moonlit trudge through the snow – have not been honored.

True friends are forgiving, and will drop everything to go for a walk.

January 23: **Adulthood**

An incident a while ago, taking my mother grocery shopping. She was then in her late 70s and her eyesight had already deteriorated. Grocery shopping takes time. She likes to know what is on the labels of what she buys. Everything that is on the labels.

I thought I would get some dog food for our new puppy. As I paused at the pet food section I could hear her voice, very clear, over the hum of other shoppers. "Now, remember! Don't overfeed him! He'll just throw up all over the rug."

I was 48 years old. But I was stopped short,

hand on a package of puppy chow. It took a few minutes for me to go on, and even longer to laugh about it.

Adulthood is a fragile condition. Childhood is always calling us to return.

January 24: **Justice**

I am intimidated by rich people. I don't know many and the ones I do know have no need to impress me. I am already nervous enough, at parties, feeling my lack of power and success.

I try to treat them as well as poor people. I try not to lump them together, as if they all disapproved of single mothers who receive social assistance. I'm sure they don't. I'm sure they're just as complex and varied a group as everyone else.

But something inside me, when I'm with them, wants to climb on the table and shriek, "Let's reform the tax system so it's fair to the poor, let's stop deferring corporate taxes..."

I suppose it would wreck the party.

January 25: **Spoiling yourself**

A day to be excessively kind to oneself is not to be taken lightly. Magazines that line supermarket checkouts have suggestions, but it takes serious thinking to take a January Rehabilitation Day.

Consider the following:

- Eat breakfast in bed, and read the paper with a second cup of coffee. (For days when you have time for only a small indulgence.)
- Eat breakfast in bed and start in right away to read a long complex novel by an author you like. (For days when you have time for more indulgence.)
- Go out, buy a brand-new hardcover copy of the latest work by an author you like, don't wait for the paperback. Put it beside your bed. The next morning, have breakfast in bed, stay in bed all day and read the novel, cover to cover. (For days when you really, really need cheering up.)

Sometimes we have to feed the decadent one within. Otherwise it grows hungry and eats us up, like a shark left unfed in a public swimming pool.

January 26: **Advice**

A friend celebrated turning 50 by asking a circle of companions at her party, "What advice do you have for me at this momentous time in my life?"

The answers were witty and generous and thoughtful. Especially those offered by teenagers, so wise in the ways of transition. That is what adolescence is about.

Humility is a useful virtue. With one quiet question, she reversed the usual dynamic of our lives. The youngest offered advice, the oldest listened carefully. We were all amazed.

Maturity is being utterly interested in what others have to teach us.

January 27: **Time**

Much popular advice says we should savor the moment, live in the now.

Maybe sometimes.

Certainly we are never more fully human than when we are absorbed in a task so compelling we no longer notice what day it is. We lose all sense of time in weaving, sanding a piece of furniture, baking bread, tilling a garden, painting a room, reading to a child.

But when we live in the past, reflecting, revisiting, this, too, is wondrously human – this ability to consider both our personal history and our collective one, and to see how the two interact.

And every year at this time, I spend part of my day in the future, making lists from seed catalogues, walking through a summer garden no less lovely because it hasn't grown yet.

Time is flexible. It runs forward and backward, and we can visit wherever we like.

January 28: **Shadow**

Sometimes I dream of sharks, robbers, floods, fire, nuclear holocausts.

A lot of violence for a nice woman.

Fierce creatures and wicked people invading

our dreams can mean our interior is trying desperately to compensate for a too-sweet exterior. Humans are not meant to be always smiling.

We are meant to be honest. Whole people, with dark and light sides showing. The problem with always being nice is the other side grows and grows. It takes more and more energy to keep it hidden, until finally something snaps. We get sick, or explode at someone passing by, or we turn the shadow-energy inward and become depressed.

A shark is a lady's best friend. If one appears in your dream, ask it what it wants.

January 29: **Perfectionism**

Getting ready for a dinner party can unleash the worst part of me. I scurry around cleaning house, inwardly cursing my family, sweeping up balls of dog hair, vainly attempting to scrub off those little rust rings that grow on the bathtub when people leave the shaving cream can in a puddle of water.

If I nag too much, the family melts away,

finding necessary things to do. Perhaps they will be put off dinner parties forever.

The thing is, no guest as far as I know has ever crawled around looking for dog hair or taken a bath at a dinner party.

Dinners were intended to be enjoyed by candlelight. Dim candlelight.

January 30: **Growing old**

My mother sometimes brings a group of her friends for tea. I am struck by how they live, these old women, loving the simplest aspects of life. Observing them, I realize I can never believe life becomes less precious as you age. It does not. Life grows no less precious and rare even marked by aching limbs and tentative vision.

This is an insight our culture will tempt me to forget.

January 31: **Justice**

None of us can live happily in a culture of injustice. We will have terrible dreams in which our teeth fall out. I dreamed once my mouth was filled with orange peels, so I couldn't utter a word. Such dreams point out the condition of our lives when we fail to speak the words we should.

We will have dreams that indicate, in the graphic way dreams have, that we fail to see. We will be in a car driven by a blind driver; or a bus, similarly guided, to show collective blindness.

When we take the rest we need, turning inward and searching our individual soul for long periods of time, we might be tempted to forget that the world also needs and calls us. Justice and spirituality are inseparable. One without the other is not complete.

FEBRUARY

February 1: **Spiritual hope**

I was a little girl who talked to trees.

Some First Peoples regard the land as the womb that gives them life. When I am with Native people, I know that little girl knew something the grownup almost forgot: how to be grateful for the gifts of wood and stone and all the small creatures that keep the soil sweet.

So, gratefully now, I strip old paint from furniture, I lug rocks around the garden, feed the worms in the compost pile. And I say thank you to the tree, the stone, the little crawling insects for the way they help the earth.

February 2: **Disagreeing with friends**

It's an art to express a different opinion from a friend's, and not harm the friendship.

Men do this well. The other night two of them, of whom I'm very fond, were discussing the economy. They have differing ideas, starting with whether it is *the deficit* or a deficit.

Both are people of integrity. But the mental frameworks with which they regard economics are miles apart.

They were very clear with each other. Each time one spoke, the other stepped into a foreign country and struggled to learn its language and customs. They took turns crossing this invisible border, listening hard, speaking carefully.

Each had as much chance of understanding what the other was saying as of learning Mandarin. But they were willing to try. And they didn't destroy their friendship.

I'm learning from this, as a woman. We don't

have to walk away from the hard stuff. Good friendships are strong enough to endure passionate opinion.

February 3: **Seeds**

Another seed catalogue arrives in the mail, a prophecy encapsulated in print and photograph, a little silent hymn to beauty.

There will be no work done for the next hour, while I live in holy ritual. I brew coffee, read, inhale scents not yet fashioned, touch petals not yet formed.

A friend will call, full of wonder. We will speak in our own peculiar tongue. This is a kind of church.

February 4: **Perfection**

"There's a crack in everything," says Leonard Cohen. "That's how the light gets in."

A woman I know is a potter, spinning bowls from tender clay. Sometimes one cracks a little in the kiln, just on the edge, a minor flaw.

Some are baptismal bowls. Should she destroy her flawed creations, she wonders, when God allows all of us, imperfect, to stay? When God loves us, beckons us to belong to God? Is she less merciful than God?

It's a thought for a February day. What flaw in my life is letting in the light?

February 5: **Waking up**

Like a coiled spring held down by the force of my waking self, memory jumps me out of sleep at three o'clock in the morning. I think of hurtful things I have said, just the day before. And my laugh, what a silly laugh it is. Shouldn't I be quiet and not laugh or speak again?

It's true, we humans cannot bear too much reality. Seeing ourselves as we really are, our faces in a photograph, our memories at three o'clock in the morning – it requires courage just to live.

But life is possible. The great mystics taught the loss of self. It is the second step in the threefold way: first, the loss of the world; then the loss of the ego, the image, the part that is in pain over the foolish remarks, the laugh.

When we are empty – and those memories that unleash themselves with such fury at three o'clock in the morning are trying to leave, to empty us – then we can receive God. Like the mystics.

The path through three o'clock in the morning winds through necessary darkness. But God is there.

February 6: **Mothers and daughters**

When we were young, the only way some mothers knew how to care for some of us was by nagging. They lived in a different time; most women had less power, it was all they knew to do.

They loved us. They did the best they could. Sometimes it was wonderful, sometimes awful.

We try not to do the same thing with our own daughters. We will do better. And because we live in this time, with its busy careers and steady bombardment of items to desire, we will also do worse.

It takes a lot of strength to just make our own mistakes, and not repeat the mistakes of others.

February 7: **Faith**

Sometimes I manage to live full of assurance that I am deeply loved by God. Mostly, though, I lose it, battered by the world. On Sunday I struggle back to church, hoping to be told that yes, indeed, God loves me unconditionally, no strings, even when I mess up.

That's what church is for.

That's why, when women gather and share food and laugh and assure each other they will be okay, it is church. Even the most secular women, when they laugh together and are healed by an accepting love, it is church.

February 8: **Making beauty**

It seems female to have such an urge for beauty we can't resist drifting around rooms or office, tidying, adding a cushion, a bit of green.

Wherever we are has to have ourselves grown into it, as if the boundaries between us and the outer world are less distinct than between men and their world. We spill over into it, and absorb it into us, with such ease.

We are learning, we women, to define ourselves, to have edges. That's good. But I hope I never forget I am part of the ordinary physical world around me, releasing its beauty without thought. The world is in itself lovely; it only desires to be seen.

February 9: **Rage**

The link between ourselves and country is complicated. I am affected by what touches others in my country. If bad public policy means hungry children, I write letters, I am argumentative – a big step for a shy person.

When the winds of transition blow away from my view of history, I am discouraged.

So I cultivate my garden. It's what Voltaire said we should do. Many thought him cynical for that, and perhaps he was. It is not cynicism, though, but hope that sends me out to see how life insists on being born, how every nasturtium, every earwig has an irresistible urge to live. When it's hot and dry, the petunias hunker down and wilt to conserve water, rising miraculously when conditions are better.

I learn from them. Their stubborn force leaches into me. I dig, weed, water, rest myself, am made hopeful by Creation's strength.

February 10: **Weeping**

Sometimes I sit in church and cry. I'm not sure why. It has something to do with being ambushed by emotion that comes up behind me suddenly while I am listening to the sermon or the children's choir.

In the Eastern Orthodox tradition, I am told, tears are a sign of the presence of God. Perhaps that's why I weep when small children bravely sing songs with words larger than themselves. They say more of holiness than they imagine, inviting God's presence for us all.

February 11: **Children**

Sometimes children appear in our dreams. It's best to treat such dreams as if a real child had turned to us, honoring us with a gift of sudden, unsolicited trust.

Such dreams describe our creations, an act of hospitality, a part in a play, a blossoming friendship. Whatever has life in us and grows.

We can ask our dream-children their name and what they need. Sometimes they will answer.

February 12: **Belief**

It's a terrible mistake to wrap up spirituality in a set of rules. They just beg to be overturned. The other day a woman told me she had forgiven Jesus for only stating one half of the equation, for only calling God Father, instead of Mother sometimes too. He was a child of his culture, she said.

It pleased me to see her turn things upside down. Her suggestion that the one who teaches us everything about forgiveness needs also to be forgiven, is so fresh.

I yearn for that newness. When anything, the tenets of feminism as well as of religious tradition, becomes rule-bound, we want to challenge it. Eve reaching for apples, feeling their tender skin...Women can think for themselves.

February 13: **Sacredness of children**

The world is sacred, not only charged with God's glory, but holy in itself.

This is not to deny the presence of evil, which I contemplate as fully as I can and still stay sane. There is evil in public policy which fails to protect children, forcing some into substandard housing or to a foodbank.

The evidence of evil is clear without spelling out the details.

But God walks here and loves this place and calls God's beloved creatures to create a home. Not in heaven (although maybe that, too) but on earth. An earth where there are no school pizza days unless every child can enjoy them, and no school trips unless every child can afford to go.

Women know, of all things in this holy universe, nothing is more sacred than a child.

February 14: **Sadness**

There are times when we are simply sad. Something dark has swum up through the fissures of our soul. It often happens in middle age. We grow strong enough to be sad. The soul waits until we have friends and the strength of maturity to suggest we do our inner work. Inexplicable sadness is just calling us to grow up whole at last.

February 15: **Waking up**

When things happen so fast in life we can't think them through during the day, they come back at night and wake us up. The human spirit wants to understand. We are self-conscious creatures.

This makes us tired the next day, so the pace of life grows more harried, and then we need even more to wake up at night in order to think about the things we don't have time to think about during the day.

Going to bed in early evening helps. If the psyche wants time, we can help it. We can sleep awhile, wake up in the quiet middle of the night, and do the required reflecting.

February 16: **Feeding birds**

Life seems fragile these cold, short days. The maple that shelters my window looks dead. There is nothing to prove that anything in this frozen landscape will ever be green again.

Except the chickadees, grosbeaks, blue jays, munching at the feeders on their way from one place to another. I fill the trays with tiny black Niger seed for the chickadees, sunflower seeds for the grosbeaks, peanuts for the jays. And squirrels.

They ornament the trees with reassuring life. Even when they chatter and fight among themselves, their presence is reward enough.

We know the mind of God, feeding birds.

February 17: **Work**

I belong to the first generation of women to need a career for self-acceptance as well as cash. Women are expected now to be as successful as men in collecting honors, degrees, promotions.

I have no argument with this. We needed to become assertive, independent, articulate, confident; we have done that, and not easily.

But we also require the clarity to know this does not define us. We are more than our work. We are more than our children, mates, houses, though all these may be precious.

What is essential is something else, only glimpsed in what we dream and in what makes us weep and laugh. Some call it soul.

What we do can never define who we are.

February 18: **Personal myth**

We make ourselves a story to get through life. It's a bit of fiction that aims at truth and often finds some. But the creature cannot have the complex eye of the Creator. We see only our reflection.

No matter. A story is a fine thing in itself.

Sometimes the story is interrupted by a cry of anguish and our ceaseless, inner storyteller pauses in her tale. A main character in the story departs, or the heroine experiences massive failure. Then the plot falters – especially if the inner myth describes a woman-who-can-do-anything.

It's all right. The storyteller will not be beheaded, especially not if she can weave that cry into her story. The myth will contain more truth than before.

Wholeness comes from witnessing our pain and seeing our real self, even for a moment, with love.

February 19: **Falling in love**

An excellent descriptive phrase, falling in love. It conveys that old joke about the optimist who falls out a 14th-storey window, and is heard to say, as he hurtles past a sixth-storey balcony, "So far, so good!"

Most of us fall uncontrolled and wrapped in hope.

There's more to it than that, though. Falling in love teaches us more about ourselves than any other experience, except that of hating. It's because we love or detest what resides, in some infinitesimal way, inside ourselves. We hate because we see our own greed, ignorance, spitefulness on someone else's face. We love because we touch in someone else a palpable echo of our own goodness, compassion, wisdom – virtues scarcely known within us, yet longing to be seen.

February 20: **Saying nothing**

One of the most valuable conversational skills I know is saying nothing.

With our children for example. Sometimes they tell us things, everything from what they plan to do with their lives to how they will spend the evening. We may see flaws in their reasoning; but unless those plans are health-threatening to themselves or others, it's nearly always best to let our children arrive at their own insights. They'll figure out how life works, that way. And with luck, they may allow you into their reflection process later.

Or our friends. Unless they ask for advice genuinely and directly, it's much better not to give it. There's the possibility it might be good advice for us, but not for them. There's the possibility it might be very good advice for them, but since their own mother always gave them unsolicited advice, they may resist it now because they couldn't resist it when they were children.

True wisdom says, "Mmm, interesting," from time to time, but does not impose itself unless requested.

February 21: **Male wisdom**

Some women display a permanent rage toward men in general. Many of us are damaged by individual men and many are abused by systems dominated by males.

But that doesn't mean the entire principle of maleness is rotten. As a species, men and women have far more in common than we have separating us, and we understand and participate in one another's ways of being more than we know. We need each other.

Once, before an important trip which had me terrified, I dreamed of a tough old male reporter. The dream figure, unfamiliar to me, spoke confidently about how good a reporter I was, told me how to handle the story. That dream stayed with me for the whole assignment.

I needed a male principle, found within me, to survive. Male wisdom is as valuable as our own. We do ourselves damage if we fail to recognize it in ourselves or in others.

February 22: **Perfect mother**

Nobody can be the perfect mother, there are no experts in mothering, it's too mysterious. I know mothers who have done all the right things, and ended up with enormous pain in their family life. And I know mothers who did all the wrong things, and whose children are patient with them and love them to distraction.

Raising children is a great mystery, a voyage into the unknown. We shouldn't feel bad if we end up on the rocks as parents at some point. Most of us spend some time there.

February 23: **God**

Looking for clues about our God, we tell stories. One of my favorites is the story of the Babylonian exile, in which the Israelites (it doesn't matter who we are, in these stories the Israelites are us) are led away as captives, and then called home by God after 50 years of mournful life in Babylon.

And there is the one about the prodigal son. He was called home, remember, by his self-inflicted misfortune and received by his father with joy.

I need these stories in which God is the generous father, not the stern judge who needs a price to be paid before forgiveness. That's the one we hear most often, in which Jesus dies to save us.

When I am at odds with someone, and feel exiled from their love, I need to hear instead how God the loving parent always wants to restore our world to harmony and peace.

Sometimes all we want is to come home.

February 24: **Connections**

I talk a lot to the man who built my house. This is a feat; I never met him. The building is 90 years old and he's dead.

I tell him how I like the way he put big windows facing south, looking over the backyard and the boulders he hauled to one side. I've turned them into rock gardens. I like the way the streetside windows, facing north, are careful and infrequent. It's as if he knew that almost five decades later there would be traffic here and the house would want to look south, not ignoring the street exactly, just treating it with diffidence.

I love the turn of the stairway, the angle of the sun through the windows in the evening, and I tell him so. I thank him for the maple he planted.

His life affects mine deeply. And we never met.

This is the meaning of history. It's true for houses and nations. We are absolutely connected to the past, to people we have never met, but with whom we share geography.

There is always a cloud of witnesses around us. It is wise to nod to them occasionally.

February 25: **Approximate justice**

Like everything else, justice is seldom perfect. (For example, author Marie Fortune – whose work on sexual abuse issues, especially within churches, has been groundbreaking – says that women who have been harassed must often settle for approximate justice. "Victims deserve more," she says, "but should at least receive approximate justice.") Women need to be able to go through life knowing what justice is, reaching for it for ourselves and others. But life comes in a flawed container for everyone. The ability to live with a certain amount of ambiguity is a useful tool for life.

A wise woman fights for justice and accepts life at the same time.

February 26: **Jacob**

We find ourselves in stories. I am always surprised at how I find myself in stories where men are the main characters.

Jacob, for example – he who wrestled with the angel, or God, or whoever that late-night visitor was. He struggled all night and was not beaten. He didn't win either; he just hung in there fighting, surviving, not giving up, just holding his ground until dawn. The way women do. That's why I like him. He reminds me that just holding on can be a form of victory.

February 27: **Friends**

Before we can be a good friend to someone else, we need to be well acquainted with ourselves.

To be a good friend is to have empathy – the ability to leave one's own problems and passions and enter fully into the problems and passions of the other.

It's like being a time traveler. It ought to be impossible, especially since we have to keep a rope attached to our own self. Entering another's problems is not helpful unless we can bring our own perspective to bear.

If I have no foundation or strength or identity of my own, I am useless to my friend. One of two things will happen. I might enter into her life, but have no connection with my own life experience to draw on for help. There will be no exhilarating moment of clarity when we can see front and back of the difficulty, because we have two sets of eyes.

The other possibility is that I will – perhaps wisely – not enter her life in any depth. Without a strong identity of my own, I might not find my own self again. A time traveler without a rope.

Write in a journal. Pray. Finding out who we are is how we learn to be a friend.

February 28: **Angels**

American theologian Walter Wink tells us there is an ethos, an angel belonging to every institution. He explains this with John's letters to the "angels of the churches " in the Book of Revelations.

I love his idea, that places have angels. Once, a tall young man stopped by my house and told us he used to live here with six siblings.

Those children made an energy that's more than mortar and brick. There is a good angel here. When we first moved in, for example, a group of South Africans touring Northern Ontario came for music and dancing and African food. The angel of the house loved it. It expanded visibly to encompass that celebration.

The angel of the house loves the notes my daughter leaves around the kitchen, and the magazines that cover every level surface, and the dog, and the phone ringing when the older kids come home from college. The smell of coffee. Company. The angel of this house offers sympathy when I am up past midnight with a deadline.

This house, like every house, is filled with presence. And this presence, this angel, is not fixed, it is potential.

The angel of an institution can be addressed, says Wink. Something to consider. If the angel of a house, or workplace, is not helpful but annoying, it can be called to change. That is the nature of angels.

February 29: **Heaven**

It's important to think critically about our faith. Jesus' command to "Become as a little child" has been understood to mean we should stop thinking and trust whatever anyone tells us.

But everyone knows that's the most dangerous thing a child can do.

It's that way for children of the faith as well. Women know well the price we have paid for being too trusting of the patriarchs – centuries of being saint or prostitute, virgin or virtuous wife. None are whole people, only flat caricatures, some without light, some without shadow.

Heaven is also something to think about with care. Are we intended to suffer through this life, with our reward to follow? ("Pie in the sky when you die," according to some not especially taken by this view.) Or is earth where heaven can be glimpsed and sought for, a place where we fight to make things right?

MARCH

March 1: **Transformation**

Great changes occur, at times, in our relationship with God. Not easily, of course. We suffer sickness or grief, we have strange dreams, and then one day, in the midst of our brokenness, there is a sliver or a burst of light. God is closer than before.

This rhythm of wondering darkness and light to follow is what faith is about. Sundays we seek transformation – the turning of our souls toward God. We sift the Christian story for it, reenacting year by year the pain and exaltation of the birth, the death, the resurrection.

This month or next, for almost the 2000th time, we will recount once more how Jesus died, how the body was placed in a tomb Joseph had recently dug out of solid rock. Later, as startled as if we had never heard it before, we will sing again the story of Jesus rising transformed from that hollow dark place.

It's God who does the transforming. Knowing that may help us survive our necessary times of darkness. We cannot fight our Good Fridays, our own descent into the underworld. But we can trust we will arise, closer than before to the God who makes with holy purpose both radiance and tomb.

March 2: **Inner work**

Who would have thought
It would be so grim
To scan the heart
  Within

Who would have dreamed
There'd be this mess

Here inside all
  Darkness

I wouldn't have sought these dragons
Unattended
I hoped that I might enter here
  Befriended

I should have known I only
By myself and quaking

Can kiss these claws
And set me free
The me my self am
  Making.

March 3: **Friends**

The hardest thing about moving is leaving good friends. We simply don't let them go, of course. We stay in touch, write, visit, phone. This is a great pleasure.

When we move again, we have two sets of close friends to write, visit, phone, plus the new ones in the new town, because who can live without friends close at hand. And then if we move again...

Nourishing friendship requires energy. It's not work in any usual sense, more like gardening, hours uncounted by delight. But lack of time limits intimacy. Anyone can have any number of warm acquaintances, but friendship is different.

It may be necessary to move. But we should count the cost, reckon the sacrifice, and lament. Mourning undone reappears as depression or rage.

March 4: **Wise women**

My maternal grandmother arrives in my dreams, sometimes in a form I scarcely remember. She'll be younger than I am now, hair coiled in heavy blond braids on top of her head, and lovely.

I am alert for what she has to say. My grandmother came from Scotland, alone, at 16, to start a new life.

Women did that in those days. I can't imagine having that kind of courage. But I know when she appears, I am being assured; whatever lies ahead, the resources I need are within, embedded in my genes and carried in memory and the whole long narrative of my family.

The wisdom of the women in our dreams is our own.

March 5: **Home**

Women are far from home, refugees in a strange land where what you buy is more important than how you are.

We live in a land where whether we are thin or fat, well-dressed or not, is of paramount importance, and where girls begin to diet when they are ten or 11.

This is not our true home.

To be a woman is to be strong enough to give birth to a child or an idea. It's to be strong enough to defend that child (whether it's a human child, or an idea.) Being thin has little to do with that.

We need to remember our true home.

March 6: **Jacob**

The stories that make their way into the holy books of any faith are there because they illuminate something about us.

Jacob, for instance. He, again, who wrestled with the angel. He (male) teaches me (female) about identity. He struggled and was wounded and received a new name. Israel.

It's what women do. We struggle with relationships and money and kids and inevitably we are wounded. But if we are wise and lucky we will discover who we are: strong and separate, interdependent and caring, limping perhaps, like Jacob, but whole in ourselves. We will be named – the song goes – Woman.

Forging this identity takes time. It was likely a long night for Jacob, too.

March 7: **Media**

Some writers have scant compassion for churches. I wonder about this. It may be that the skepticism required for writing militates against the too-willing trust some churches want.

Or maybe skilled attunement to the society around them, which writing needs, leads some to play out that culture's repression of spirituality. What we fear, we repress. Our world's pursuit of wealth above compassion is challenged by faith's assertion that God will strike down the mighty.

The eyes of faith read between the lines. If a writer seeks only to preserve the status quo, read carefully.

March 8: **Authority**

Sometimes I teach Creative Writing in the evenings. The first session is difficult; I come home and go to bed and try to sleep. But a sneering inner voice keeps me awake. "Who do you think you are, woman?" it says. "You don't know from nothing about writing."

"I know a little about life," I say meekly. "A little about people."

The voice cackles. "Enough to know you can't teach. *Hahahaha*."

I don't sleep. I go over what I said, what each student said. I get up and write down what I will say next week to correct the impression I have made this week.

I am not alone in my fear. It's easy for us women to undermine our own authority, to believe we have none. Many of us raise our voices at the end of sentences in a peculiar interrogative indicating we stand to be corrected. We defer to men in meetings, adding our voices only after they have had their say. We avoid microphones.

It's no wonder. The voice of our culture has fiercely obscene nicknames for women. "Know your place," it says softly.

But that voice can be silenced. I just keep teaching, my students are loyal, something must be right. The voice gets quieter as the weeks go by.

The best authority comes from within, independent from the world, tested and proven by our own experience.

March 9: **Sacred meals**

Christmas dinner, the first time in years all the

brothers and sisters were together at the same time. Or the first meal after the baby came home, the one that came early and almost didn't make it.

The lunch with the friend, when you thought the friendship was over, and it wasn't.

The kids bringing breakfast in bed. The last birthday party when Grandpa was alive.

Bacon on a campfire, work falling away, the summer stretching ahead.

No wonder there are stories where people discover they have shared their meal with a god: Jesus, breaking bread on the road to Emmaus; the Greek legend of Baucis and Philemon with the endlessly flowing pitcher of milk.

Hospitality, the welcoming of others, also welcomes the divine.

March 10:
Grandmothers, daughters, granddaughters

"Do you mind," my 12-year-old daughter says, as we get into the car after dropping off Grandma and her groceries, "if I just scream for a minute?"

She has guided Grandma through the store and read her labels. She has listened to advice and carried her groceries and hugged her goodbye. She loves her Grandma with an unreserved, heart-tugging affection, but those labels have almost pushed her over the edge. "Sure," I say. And we both scream, in the middle of the traffic, for a full minute. Then we giggle the rest of the way home. "I love Grandma a lot," I say to her. "I love her because she is my mother, and because I know she loves us more than anything. But sometimes I think reading her labels may drive me crazy."

"Thanks for not doing that to me," says my daughter, mindful of the future.

"I'll find something. Don't worry," I say.

Exasperation and love both come from the same crowded place in our hearts.

March 11: **Angels**

Some people, especially children, see angels. Or they hear them, an indescribable music of the spheres that draws us into the divine.

We live in a culture ambivalent about angels, turning them into lapel pins or greeting cards on the one hand, ignoring them on the other; seldom acknowledging them as messengers from God.

They deserve better of us. Their concern for us softens our hard edges in an age marked by meanness. Even if we can't see them, we can encourage the angel of our dwelling to be hospitable and warm, perhaps a little messy with papers and books and plants. Even at our most binary, we can look up from our computers and VCRs and welcome something living.

And we can be alert for these messengers when they appear: the figure in a dream who offers wisdom, the stranger who surprises us with unsolicited generosity, the song that has us weeping in the car on the way to work. The world is jammed with meaning, overflowing with it. But we have to listen carefully and offer it a name. Angels will do fine.

The universe is always telling us we are beloved.

March 12: **Justice note**

We fall in love with a certain place. As children we would write our name and then our address, beginning with the street and ending triumphantly with world, universe. We give ourselves a specific place in the cosmos.

So I am located in northern Ontario, not far from a lake, Ojibway territory. The area I can cover on foot or bicycle is where I most truly live.

Still, I cherish other parts of Canada. One child was born in Quebec, one lives in British Columbia, dear friends inhabit other provinces. I have lived the history of this whole country. I am Canadian. So I yearn for its wholeness, as I do for any part of me. I long for justice like a mighty river, setting everyone free.

Spirituality is a journey outward as well as inward.

March 13: **Grace note**

The moment every parent dreads. Our 17-year-old daughter is taking the family car for the weekend, driving hundreds of miles with two friends.

Somewhere, out of the depths of my fear come these words. "You might have an accident. If you do, remember, the only thing that matters is that you three are safe. It doesn't matter about the car. You are all we care about. If anything happens, and the car is wrecked, don't even think about the car." (Which still has a year of payments left to make on it, but never mind, what is all that insurance for, I thought but didn't say.)

My daughter's hug was enough.

If, by some miracle, we find the right words before we even need them, it's wise to say them out loud.

March 14: **Giving advice**

I love seeing and hearing good women friends in conversation. There's sometimes a moment when several friends have been together for awhile talking and you remember how much you trust each other. One woman asks another for advice. Genuinely asks, not just out of politeness.

And the other counters, first of all: "Well, what do you think, yourself?"

The most amazing thing happens. Especially if all present are patient and wait quietly. The one who asked the question, who needs the advice, begins to draw the necessary wisdom up out of herself. She thinks out loud. The other listens carefully and affirms the best parts, adding humbly to the delicate nest of thought that is being built. The original thinking, though, arises out of the soul of the person who needs it. And so it is the best advice for her.

Onlookers should hold their collective breath and be still. If all goes well, they may add their own bits of feathers and twigs, always diffidently, never investing their own ego in another's life. Recognizing and naming another's own inner wisdom is one of the purer forms of love.

March 15: **Unbalanced life**

Even without knowing it, humans have an extraordinary ability to compensate for incongruity between their inner and outer existence. The body knows when the soul is saying something different from the mind, and pushes for harmony.

But I also believe that when we have been balanced for a long time, God or the universe whacks us into chaos for awhile, so we can see a new direction.

Our souls need risk. When we get too comfortable and stop challenging ourselves, an angel arrives to shake things up. Not so we will need God (I don't believe God is so hungry for affection) but so we will see the world afresh.

March 16: **Companionship**

A friend can't do therapy. We make ourselves dependent on a therapist, while we leave adulthood to begin again. Friendship can't be asked to carry such a weight.

A friend can be something as valuable as a therapist, though. A companion, someone who walks beside, so we are not alone. Not powerful, not learned, just the one who is there when the tears come. A good friend is not afraid to go with us into the dark.

March 17: **Healers**

Some people, I am told, have a natural capacity to heal others with touch or prayer. And others, maybe all of us, have healing power we could develop.

The important ingredient is "loving intentionality."

This explains why I hover day after day over my seedlings and why even those that have to spend a good part of their young lives in a north window in March still grow up strong.

We shouldn't discount the power of our love.

March 18: **Anointing**

I'm not sure baby oil does much for the baby itself. But lovingly smoothing on oil does wonders for the love between parent and child.

There is the same power at the other end of life in the anointing of one who is dying.

Even a hand quietly held for a moment can be a gift of energy and blessing. The power of human touch is immeasurable.

March 19: **Manipulation**

We all have moments when we're backed into a corner, where our words or actions will be twisted and used against us.

The more innocent we are, the less used to manipulation as a tool, the more likely we are to be trapped.

We need to keep telling the truth. We need to not blame ourselves and to disentangle ourselves from the manipulative one. Refusing communication is not lack of compassion. Loving your enemies doesn't mean you have to take their phone calls.

March 20: **Men**

Women shouldn't ignore what we can learn from male attitudes toward the world. We've spent most of 2000 years being the second sex, so there are a few useful characteristics we didn't have a chance to develop.

While we were socialized to be quiet, men were encouraged to express opinions. Even now, passion in the voice of a female speaker can lead to charges of stridency. While we were educated in looking after details (how many for supper, what will we give them?) men were taught to see the big picture.

It'll take a long time to change the world. It doesn't hurt to try on men's vision sometimes, and see what they see.

March 21: **Time**

Women's time is precious. Women's work is important. In our various incarnations, we have careers and raise children and cook and garden and listen to music and read the paper. Some even do all of the above.

One of the things women can learn from men is the way they handle the telephone. Few men will allow themselves to have their day nibbled away by phone calls.

"Boundary" is not a bad word. It's something you put around yourself in order to have a life. It's all right to turn the phone off sometimes.

March 22: **Dependence**

Biology does make a difference. It's usually women who take time away from a career to have a child, for example. And then we have to figure out how to raise it.

It's complicated. Listening to those who have no words. Listening for our dreams to tell us when we are being too rigid or too soft. It's like learning to paddle a canoe, knowing when to slide along with the wind and when to head for shore, knowing "control" is not the word for this.

Taking time to do that learning means a time of financial dependence on our partner, or, if a single parent, on the community around us. A time of being financially dependent on another is not easy. But we can learn humility and an identity that comes from who we are and not what we can buy. And compassion for those who have no choice but dependence all their lives.

March 23: **Interdependence**

What do we owe to our spouses, children, parents? What do we owe our vocations, our solitude, our selves? Words like independence and dependence, autonomy and intimacy leap off the pages of textbooks and into our lives.

Interdependence is a useful one to add to the list. In our house, I am the gardener, my husband the undergardener – mixing compost, hauling manure and dead foliage, cutting the lawn, which yearly becomes a smaller portion of the yard. I design flowerbeds. He complains and digs them.

It's a congenial arrangement, balanced by his ability to be the chief creator of a social life around us, and his exquisite skill in a crisis, when I prefer to hide under the bed.

We compensate for each other's strengths and weaknesses. Interdependence in marriage is when each is in charge of her or his life – and at the same time, each life is deeply entwined with the other.

March 24: **Animals**

When my father died one November night many

years ago, we had already begun the two-hour drive north. Home. We didn't know. But as we drove the dark highway under a cold moon, we saw little puffs of what seemed to be smoke preceding us. And then we saw a deer, racing along the road beside the car, her visible breath hanging for a moment behind her in the chill air.

The deer accompanied us for what seemed a long time.

We got home too late to say goodbye. But the deer had leapt beside us just in the moments of my father's dying.

I believe that white-tailed deer is my totem. She had appeared in my dreams before, and she still does. She is wise and gentle. Most times, she offers a new, scarcely-touched path and the offer of accompaniment – just as she did that cold November night.

There is an animal mentor for each of us.

March 25: **Sensitivity**

To live a full life it's important to have a thin skin, to feel what others feel, and to care about that.

To survive life with integrity, it's important to have a thick skin, to be brave enough to tell the truth no matter what rage and hurt feelings will follow.

This is a difficult balance to strike. It's sometimes helpful to ask, "Is this something I will go to the wall for?" We can only deal with the tough stuff on so many fronts at once.

March 26: **Gardens**

This is the month I ferret around in a closet and find a box of dried-up geraniums. I yank them out, cut them back almost to the roots, stick them in pots of soil, water them, and put them in the window.

In a week or so, out of the dead brown stem, new leaves appear. By the end of May, they are full and green and covered with blossoms.

This is against logic, to be revived by sun and water after months of neglect. It fills me with hope. The earth prefers life over death.

March 27: **Dancing**

My mother has taken up aerobic exercise. She is 83, and can't see. I trust, although I have no evidence, that these exercises are geared to someone her age.

She came to dinner a few Sundays ago, as is her habit. After dinner she got up from the table and demonstrated line dancing.

I have never seen my mother dance before.

I conclude from this that her soul wants to go on growing. Surely dancing is an activity that comes from some deep and ancient and lovely human part of us, and surely that part is the soul. Her soul has no concept of age or death.

Immortality may not be given to the body, but clearly it is given to the spirit.

March 28: **Generativity**

When our oldest son was very young he fell in love with our neighbor, Stephanie. She was then in her late 70s. He was not yet in his teens. From her, he developed a passion for languages. She spoke seven. He decided to learn Polish –

Stephanie had grown up in Cracow – and so she taught him enough to begin a conversation with any startled Pole he happened to meet.

They talked for hours, about her life as a young woman, about history, languages, music, philosophy, religion. We teased him about learning Polish so he could become the next Pope. He considered Judaism, so deep was his love for the woman all our children came to call their Jewish grandmother.

Now, because of her, his apartment echoes with classical music, his grown-up life is carried on in a variety of tongues. Perhaps the germ of his master's degree in political philosophy began in those animated conversations.

A few months ago she died. Her life continues in all of us who felt her vivid joy in our presence.

I would like to be like her – generative. This is what is meant by generativity: the infusing of later generations with our own hard-earned wisdom, making their lives richer.

March 29: **Healing and cure**

My brother is blind. He has *retinitis pigmentosa,* an illness for which there is no cure.

My brother is, however, healed. He lives a life filled with spirituality, meaning, loved friends, work. He is valuable. He is a grandfather, an artist, a volunteer in his community so generous with his time and prodigious with his talent that he was named volunteer of the year and introduced to the Ontario legislature while all stood and clapped.

We can sometimes be cured of what ails us, sometimes not. But when we live close to God, we can be healed.

March 30: **Resurrection**

In my church at the beginning of Lent, we ceremoniously pack away all the "Alleluias." During worship, children gather up little pieces of paper with just that one word written on them, and watch carefully while they are placed in a box, and the lid taped on tight. For the next 40 days we sing no celebration songs. No alleluias. They have all been packed away.

And then comes Easter morning. The tape is ripped off the box. "Christ the Lord is risen today," we sing, "Alleluia."

Death is not the end of life, not for Jesus and not for us. Not even when we feel that we have died in the midst of life, not even when we have lost our job or our lover or our faith.

Our Creator stays with us through every kind of death. Alleluia!

March 31: **Mediators**

Jungian analyst Toni Wolff said that some women are peculiarly gifted in connecting others to their own soul. Such women are also attuned to the spirit of the earth, and can help others know what that is.

If this is true, if we are able to relate at a deep level to nature, then we also have a responsibility to articulate her pain.

What if the earth has no voice but ours?

APRIL

April 1: **Robbers and monsters**

Sometimes I am pursued by robbers. I run through hallways, struggling to escape through doors, windows, narrow spaces. It's all in my dreams, but the drift of adrenalin jolts me wide awake.

Others report dreams of fierce wild animals and dragons.

The great advantage of dream-robbers is that, unlike in waking life, you can talk to them. They are, after all, in your dream.

Paper and pencil in hand we can imagine ourself back into the dream. But instead of running, we can turn and question what scares us. "What is your name?" is a good opener.

In the course of the dialogue (written down as it unreels) we may find out what's robbing our time and energy, what's overpowering us, what memories have a hold on us.

That's a beginning to releasing their hold. In dreams as in the rest of life, good communication helps. Sometimes dragons turn into kittens when we greet them.

April 2: **Dragons**

Why so hot
I came to see
Now settle down
Don't breathe on me

I came to ask
If you could change
And what you'd be
Given a range

Of options, count them
one two three
Now bite your tongue
Don't chew on me

It's dim outside
With lowering skies
Quite dark enough to
Risk your eyes

I know – they're tender
From the flames
Here, let me touch them
See, no pain

While feathers shrink, scales
Fall away
You'll be a kitten
Born today

Come up, we'll go now
To the light
My tender little
Dragon mite

April 3: **Transformation**

Women are transformed so often. There is the change we encounter from child to woman, variously celebrated in our culture. In our house, we huffed about a suitable celebration for our daughter's first menstrual period, and she looked at us as if we were hallucinating. We retreated rapidly.

Then there is the change from woman to mother, just as final biologically and spiritually. We retrieve our waistline eventually, but our mind has changed forever. We know now why sacred texts cast God in parental terms. Theologian Marcus Borg tells us that the word for "compassion" in Hebrew and Aramaic – frequently used in relation to God – is the plural form of the word for "womb."

The medieval mystic Meister Eckhart said that God is continually giving birth to the world.

Something to ponder – women knowing the mind of God. It might help us through the sleepless nights that strike first when our children are newborns. And later, sleepless again, pacing the floor and peering out windows, wondering why the teenager isn't home yet – this is solidarity with God. God, too, worries when we are not at home, and reaches out to touch and transform us once again.

April 4: **Friends**

Sometimes we notice a crevasse has opened up in a friendship. We think we are on the same side of an issue and then discover we aren't, and then the issue gets bigger and bigger and swallows up the friendship.

It happens. Sometimes friends can agree to disagree. Sometimes, unthreatened, they can delight in arguing their way through differences again and again.

But sometimes, we just fall into a pit.

Women feel this deeply. It's wise to allow ourselves to feel the pain we are going through. It's also wise not to blame ourselves ("Oh, if only I hadn't..." or the other, "Oh, if only she hadn't...").

Relationships fail sometimes. They are hard, and we are human.

April 5: **Mothering**

Mothering might be easier if we knew that the vision we served, the hope we have for our households, was one of the Shalom – the peaceable Kingdom of God, the gentle womb of creation – not of the courtroom. Of God as the loving friend, not the bringer of punishment. God loves us whether or not we are thin, or successful, or smart, or rich or productive.

It's a thought for a spring day: what is my picture of the household of God?

April 6: **Exodus**

It's easy for women to dismiss the Bible as a patriarchal book (which it sometimes is), outdated and useless to us (which it is not).

Women have been walking such a long way, and we need to see our story laid out somewhere, in some place that time has tested. So the story of the people leaving Egypt, abandoning all their possessions and fleeing without even letting the bread rise, is the collective story of women today.

We have left our accustomed ways of thinking that held us in a form of slavery to our housework and the expectations that surrounded us as mothers, daughters, wives.

We are no longer housewives. Even those of us whose work is at home, refuse to be married to a house.

But a wilderness of too-stretched time has come instead. And the promised land is hardly visible, except sometimes in the eyes of our daughters. It was for the Israelites as it is for us. Long after the Exodus, when they were very tired, they found the Promised Land.

Part of liberation is wandering in the wilderness.

April 7: **Grace**

In case you've ever wondered what theologians mean by grace.

One day, swimming, when our first child was about four: David went out, not far, only to his waist, and we looked away for a split second. He disappeared.

His father ran to where he had been, and found him underwater, gazing up. He had slipped into a hole. Jim yanked him up and carried him coughing and sputtering back to our little collection of towels and children and frantic hugs.

As soon as he could speak, he turned to his father. "You came as fast as you could, Dad," he said.

The greatest gift is to receive what we already have.

April 8: **Identity**

There's a little dance we do with people we love. Marriage theorists describe it very well.

We pull toward one another, because intimacy, the desire to dissolve the boundaries between us, is a human desire. We sometimes see this in people who marry very young before each one's individual sense of self is sharp and clear.

But we have a corresponding human desire for identity. That pulls us back. As soon as we feel in danger of disappearing, we become distant. The dance of intimacy, marriage expert David Mace calls it.

The most powerful friendships and marriages are composed of people whose own strong and firm identities allow them to step close to each other without fear.

No wonder many of us fear intimacy with God. One could lose oneself forever in such a powerful identity. So a compassionate and lonely God yearns for us to know ourselves, to become strong, in order to draw close.

April 9: **Healing**

This time of year, plants take over the house. There are seedlings in every window. I move them from place to place, so they can share around the best light. Our bedroom, which faces south, looks like a greenhouse. "All this from such innocent little packages," a fellow gardener says in wonder, offering round a few more hundred plants than he can house.

Soon they'll go in and out, in and out, every day, getting tougher, hardening off as gardeners say, until they finally make their permanent move into the warming earth.

But this tyrannical symbiotic relationship – the plants have needs and I fill them – is powerful medicine. Maybe it's because people who work with things you can't touch – numbers, words, the insides of people's heads – are healed by the touch of earth and leaves.

April 10: **Angels**

At Kanesatake, Quebec, the place we remember in our collective history as Oka, a small group of Mohawk set up a road block to prevent a municipal golf course from expanding into their beloved pines, the green common land that held their cemetery and meeting place.

On the morning of July 11, 1990, some women and spiritual leader John Cree were saying the morning prayers. A hundred provincial police arrived to move them away and open the road. A few Mohawk warriors slipped into place, tear gas canisters were exploded by the police. Shots were fired. One policeman was killed. The origin of the bullet has never been determined.

Ellen Gabriel, a Mohawk clan mother, describes how the wind changed suddenly that morning and blew the tear gas back directly into the faces of the police. There would have been many more casualties, she says, if the "breath of our ancestors" had not come in the form of a strong and helpful breeze.

Angels are always on the side of life.

April 11: **Personality type**

One of my dearest friends is what some personality theorists refer to as a "T," a "Thinking" type. I have a large component in my psychic makeup of "F"; I am, in other words a "Feeling" type.

It's an interesting friendship. I like to talk about how this or that affected my feelings, how I "felt" this would be a good thing to do. Emotion always enters my voice.

My friend, on the other hand, thinks rather than feels her way through things, and she does it very well. While I moan about how terrible some aspect of my life is, she is quiet. When I stop, she begins, "The logical thing to do..."

I am undone.

She tells me about things in her life in a way that seems dispassionate to me. I become irate at wrongs done to her, and I rant. "You must feel awful!" I say.

She considers that carefully, thinking her way through it. "Well, yes and no," she says at last.

We rely on each other deeply. People different from ourselves help us make the best decisions.

April 12: **Work**

When a woman works very hard at a task that immerses her – a play in which she has a part, a trip she is taking with her students, an exhibition of her paintings – her own family life may suffer. Her normally placid husband may become grumpy.

This is not a conscious decision on his part. Husbands and wives and all human beings get upset when they see something outside themselves that reflects an inner trait.

A hard-working man, devoted to his career, may be afraid that if he doesn't do everything right his work will end. It's a justified fear in these days of downsizing. But he can hardly live with the idea that he is sacrificing family life to work.

So he buries that piece of self-knowledge.

But when his spouse becomes absorbed in her career as well, he has a clear opportunity to see and condemn his own harried self. It is reflected right in front of him. No wonder he gets cranky.

No marriage takes place between just two people. There are always at least two others involved – *his* unknown self, and *yours*. They talk to each other when neither of you are looking, and make trouble.

April 13: **Patience**

In 1990, in the middle of the Oka crisis as we came to call it – a Native barricade on a highway, an army, helicopters, swirling rumors – I interviewed a Native spiritual leader in his home. He knew how it all began; he lived there and he understood the hearts of the people.

Armed with my notebook, I wanted the facts. I didn't have much time, I thought.

Instead, he offered apples, the fresh fruit a kindness since we were on the wrong side of the blockade. Then he embarked on a long discussion of thankfulness, of how his people had begun that fateful day with tobacco on a sacred fire, how they thanked the Creator for all the creatures.

I wanted to know about the guns, the tear gas. Instead he listed, slowly, many creatures the Creator had made and told me all about them.

I learned patience. Finally, when he could see my white woman's inner haste had diminished enough for me to hear him, he told me all I wanted to know. Then we had coffee and talked some more. I put away my notebook.

Any dominant culture is selectively deaf to the wisdom of others. Those of us who came late to this country, who have become so numerous, have much to learn from the original people. Respect. Patience.

April 14: **Shadow**

Our shadow is the part of ourselves we bury because it is unacceptable to the culture around us. Which means there is a collective quality to it. Most of us of a certain age will have buried similar qualities.

Different generations of women face different expectations as they grow. Our shadow is created from the criticism of our parents and aunts and uncles and teachers and peers when we are young and malleable.

It requires energy to keep those qualities buried away so they can't be used. So when a woman who was taught to be a supermother stops serving perfect meals, lets the house slip and takes up painting watercolors, she will find she has more energy.

A powerhouse awaits inside us. We just have to discover our shadow.

April 15: **Eternal truths**

I love the old hymn ascribed to St. Patrick:

I bind unto myself today
the virtues of the starlit heaven,

the glorious sun's lifegiving ray,
the whiteness of the moon at even...

They knew so much, these Celtic ancestors.

Sometimes on Sunday in the church where I worship, I look out from my perch in the choir loft at the congregation. I am awed that all these people are there; that they resist this age with its speed and disenchantments to come here, into a space that exists only because people believe there is a God.

And more, a God who is bound up with "the stable earth, / the deep salt sea, / around the old eternal rocks," as the hymn continues.

Nothing could be more eternal than these faces, this yearning, this sense of the holy, passed on and on, rediscovered every generation.

When our world quakes, we can always go to St. Patrick.

April 16: **Asking advice**

The metaphor for life I like most is the hardly-new one of a journey; and the future doesn't have much in the way of maps.

But I have come to trust some things.

Like most women, I never mind asking for directions. All the life passages I have to make, from giving birth to waving goodbye to the last child, to the increasingly rapid changes in my body, have been encountered before. When I am trying to find the right thing to do, I ask other women.

April 17: **Discernment**

Discernment comes from praying over the dreams I write down. Intuition, the funny leap your mind makes when you're not looking, is tracked in dream life. Both dreams and prayer are mysterious, irrational, illogical. They can only complement the more rational step of asking experts for advice.

Finally, I discern by going as deeply as I can into the knowledge of my people. If I were Jewish, I would consult the Torah. If I belonged to some First Nations, I would go to the Medicine Wheel. For me, the journey is into scripture because its description of the territory of human existence is in a language I can read.

The way to the truth is in our own soul, in the past, in the minds of wise people, and in the mind of God.

April 18: **Anger**

So many sources for anger, and so much disapproval for women's expression of it.

We can be angry from childhood. From a perfectionism modeled by our parents and played out in our own lives. From too-rigid demands to conform. From neglect – and how is a parent struggling to balance demands of job and family to avoid some form of neglect?

Where will we let this anger express itself? In relationships, already stressed from these double loads? At the workplace? Not likely.

Better to find a loving counselor or a good workshop. Better to watch your dreams for signs. Better to divert the adrenalin of old anger into exercise.

And practice refusal. Those who have

given shape to our anger need to be refused, even if their voices are simply old tapes in our head. And practice forgiveness, the slow, difficult, loving work of forgiving oneself for not being perfect.

April 19: **Freedom**

Does Fate or God or Destiny rule our lives, or are we free to sink or swim by our own will? A hard question, and important. If life is already decided for us, why attempt change, or even make choices?

Maybe sinking or swimming is a good metaphor. Water certainly turns up in everyone's dreams. Sometimes it's a calm lake, sometimes a canal, sometimes an ocean, sometimes rains that threaten flooding. Sometimes a river.

Perhaps that balance between freedom and fate is best handled the way we would a boat, using the current when we can, not thinking we are in complete control, but not neglecting the compass and the stars either.

Life gives us tough passages. It also gives us tools.

April 20: **Writing poems**

Sometimes I sit in a circle with my friends and we read our poems to each other. We listen. There are no statements, other than the poem.

A strange thing happens. Words fill the space between us. They fling tendrils of emotion across the room, hooking them onto thin strands of logic, weaving us into a fabric so strong we can feel each other breathe.

We become beautiful to each other. This is a spiritual discipline.

Poems are like God. You can't command their presence, you can only lie down in front of where they might come, and hope they trip over you.

April 21: **Shalom**

You get a glimpse of it sitting around a table, talking, listening, laughing. Cycling with friends, paddling a canoe, snowshoeing, walking to the movies together. Comforting each other with tears.

This is the Kingdom of God Jesus talks about, just this. Amateur photographers catch it without knowing, in the smiling faces turned toward a loved friend, blowing candles.

We are the Shalom, the promised reign of God. It is here.

There are other times when we can see it: the woman in the City Council chambers, fighting for her healthy community, surely this too is the Kingdom; the teacher who sees a hungry child and starts a breakfast program; the baby thrusting itself into life in the delivery room.

Look, we are the Shalom. It is here.

April 22: **Guilt**

I live on what was once Ojibway territory. The lake I can see from my window was the route of the Voyageurs.

To be Christian, white, middle-class and North American is to inherit a history of guilt. Europeans colonized, taking Native children from their parents, taking away language and stories and songs. Some of the dances are gone forever.

I try to find a way through this, but there is none. Theologian Gregory Baum says the proper reponse when confronted with an immensity of suffering is mourning. Guilt wraps us in paralysis; mourning allows us to go on.

This is true, I believe, whether the suffering was inflicted by individuals or the blind collective will of the same ancestors who gave us free public education and the vote.

So I lament. I mourn the little ones. And I try not to make the same mistake again. The best we can take from a hurtful past is a measure of wisdom.

April 23: **Loneliness**

Sometimes in spring I stand under the apple tree and the petals fall like snow. In fall, one windy day each year, the red leaves of the maple rain down all day until finally the tree is spent – a black, many-branched trunk against the sky.

I am convinced by these blandishments that God is lonely. She needs us to see her in the silence of falling blossoms and the crunch of sun-dry leaves.

April 24: **Self-esteem**

Women's sense of worth is battered by the world. Consider the impeccable inner logic of anorexia: being fat is bad; losing weight virtuous. Therefore, the more weight you lose, the better. You die a hero's death. Women are most valuable, dead.

It's not simply the shape of our bodies. If we list all the derogatory terms we can think of for men and then do the same for women, which list is longer?

The way to self-esteem in this atmosphere is the same we offer children. We need to cherish our own imagination, just as we post children's art on our fridges.

We can listen to each other's poems, fill our homes with each other's pottery and weaving and art. This doesn't mean we have to banish the fine work of men; just give space to the imagination of women.

April 25: **Healing**

Things get disconnected that shouldn't. Medicine, for instance, got cut off from spirituality, as if our bodies could get better without our soul's participation. It's only now being reconnected.

We could look at local institutions – education, medicine, church, politics – and see what has happened to their spiritual life.

Our educational systems should honor our children's souls, not just outfit them for a life of servitude to business. Art and drama are as crucial as computers. And local politics should consider a town's quality of life, the preservation of its past and the well-being of its children, not simply the bottom line of its annual budget.

The creativity of women is expressed in our work to heal the community around us.

April 26: **Freedom**

Somehow along the way, I became a collector. Books. Cupboards to hold more books. Big pots for holding plants. Books. Plants.

Some philosophies teach the absence of desire, but I don't attempt that. I am filled with desires. What hope can there be, then?

The plants solve part of that, by multiplying so quickly they must be given away in quantity. And the books, that tempt me with their pretty covers and their wisdom? One day, perhaps, I will have learned it all. But not yet.

Freedom will come when all wisdom is carried within.

April 27: **Ambiguity**

Women are skilled at living with ambiguity. We know how to clutch two opposites and live both at the same time.

We protect our children and let them go. We cherish our identity even while we risk it in marriage. We are empathetic and surround ourselves with boundaries.

It is possible to cherish solitude and activism, peace and justice, prayer and picketing. All are needed for a full life.

April 28: **Rituals**

An illness cost the husband of a friend of mine his ability to function intellectually as an adult.

He is charming and kind. But he is brain-injured.

After a long time she made two lists: on the first, she wrote all the things her husband had been; on the second, all the things he had become. She took matches and the first list to the beach. She burned the list, and scattered the ashes in the water. With this ritual, she tried to say her goodbyes to the person he had been.

She was wise and brave, picking up the pieces of her life and beginning the necessary going-on. Rituals help us be brave like that. They name things and put a frame around one time in our life so we can gather strength to leap into the next one.

April 29: **Anger**

We learned how to express emotion by watching to see what others, our mothers perhaps, did. My own favorite expression is sulking. I developed it myself, thank you, not wishing to repeat patterns I had observed. But it is singularly useless. It is paralyzing and brings all joy in the household to a grinding halt.

I've been trying to remember a few things:

1. Begin with "I feel angry because..."
2. Keep in mind that the person you're angry with will have his or her own carefully-tooled bad habits and projections.
3. Don't blame. Say "I was hurt when..." not "You jerk, it's your fault..."
4. Listen.
5. Stay in the present. Deal with what is at hand now, not with what happened last year.
6. If you can't talk, write a letter and leave it on the fridge. If the whole family is at fault, that's where they all go eventually. Or on the pillow. The books say don't fight in the bedroom, but if you have a houseful of kids and you don't want an audience, the only other place is the bathroom with the door locked.

One gift we can give our children is the ability to deal constructively with anger.

April 30: **Prayer**

I love the way, in church, there is a discipline to the liturgy that demands we do intercessory prayer. Just for a moment we hold politicians, even the ones we detest, in the light of God. We mention them in the same breath as people who are poor or sick.

It's the only place all these people are gathered together. It's the one house where all of us are around the same table, eating the same bread, placing ourselves in the mind of the same God.

If Christianity had only this wisdom, it would be enough. Love your enemies, and pray for the welfare of all.

MAY

May 1: **Birth**

It's amazing how often most of us dream of giving birth. (Once, dreaming, I gave birth to a chicken, which was most unpleasant.)

Even men have such dreams; even women long past the age of having children.

There's always the same question to ask of the dream. "What new thing is being born in me?"

We don't always see how we are changing, growing, becoming new, giving birth to ourselves. Perhaps we are learning to laugh after a period of mourning; perhaps we are beginning to feel strong after a loss of confidence. These are matters to celebrate.

"See what is happening in you," is the constant, joyful cry of our dreams. We wouldn't want to miss all the excitement.

(And I've learned to like chicken again.)

May 2: **Hope**

I think a spiritually healthy child has a sense of hope. My daughter, cuddled in bed beside me one day as I read the Saturday paper, suddenly burst into tears. "Hole in the ozone layer," shouted the headline. "Skin cancer rising."

She is fairskinned and sometimes sunburned. And believed, in that moment, she was doomed.

The prophet Micah has a wonderful passage about this. He says the task of human beings is to seek justice, love kindness, and walk humbly with our God. That's the only hope I can give her (and me): that we have a humble God who comes to earth and lives with us and shares the sunburns and skin cancer.

And we will pray and fight together for all the subtle, intricate protections our humble Creator placed around the world She birthed.

May 3: **God**

There's a fair amount of confusion over whether God is man, woman, friend or companion, and whether God is immutable, invisible, eternal. Women have a big stake in this. God has been considered male for such a long time. The fact that women were not made in His image made us lower than the angels, and men as well.

But all that's fixed now. Well, sort of. In some circles. At a conscious level.

The fact is, it's difficult to recover fast from centuries of a God endowed only with testosterone. The image is settled in our bodies somewhere around the brainstem. It would take at least a century for us to evolve out of it, even if a lot of people weren't unwilling to give it up.

Theologian Dorothee Soelle, reaching into the mystical tradition, suggests we might think of God as light. It's not an image of dominance (how could light demand submission?) nor of one gender. "I am the light of the world" works very well.

We have nothing to think with but images. The ones we use are important.

May 4: **Novels**

Tony Hillerman's sergeant Jimmy Chee of the Navaho Police Force is learning the singing way, struggling to balance the way of his people and the way of white justice. All his work is undertaken on the knife-thin edge between the old ways and the new.

I read Hillerman and I feel less alone, more balanced, because of Jimmy Chee. There are holy texts everywhere.

May 5: **What women want**

King Arthur, inadvertently straying into a rival knight's territory, killed a deer, and therefore owed a debt of honor. In payment, the rival knight set a riddle. They were fond of riddles in those days. Within a year, King Arthur must search and discover what it is that women most desire, or be beheaded.

In the midst of his search, Arthur and his finest knight, Sir Gawain, are accosted by a hideous hag. The fearsome hags of those days could steal a man's soul, sucking it out of his body in an instant. She tells them the answer, on condition she marry Sir Gawain.

Her answer saves the King's life. The wedding, complete with bewildered guests, proceeds. After the feast, Sir Gawain escorts his bride to the wedding chamber. At her invitation, he bravely kisses her.

She immediately turns into a beautiful woman. Overjoyed at what is clearly the breaking of a spell, he holds out his arms.

"Wait," she says. "You have a choice to make. I can be a hideous hag by day and my true shape at night. Or I can be lovely in the daytime, and a hag at night. Choose."

"This choice concerns your life," he answers. "The choice is yours."

With those words, the spell placed on the

lady by her wicked uncle is shattered. She resumes her own lovely form. And she and Sir Gawain live happily ever after.

What women really want is to be in charge of our own lives.

May 6: **Work**

The kind of work many women do thrives on perfectionism. Sometimes it's necessary to give in and work and work until the filing is done, the article written, the project is completed.

But if this obsession with perfection continues, it can kill the spirit on which our work depends.

My spirit survives because of my family. They have an instinct for the moment creative focus has degenerated into blindness. They walk into my office, one at a time or together, and sit down purposefully. Just needing to be near me. Asserting their place as part of my life. The people we love save us from ourselves.

May 7: **Angels**

A wonderful, visiting aunt was telling stories about her life in the air force. She had joined during World War II, and, toward the end of the war, was given a then-new sulfa drug for an illness. She promptly fell into a coma, and stayed there for three weeks. During that time she saw an angel bathed in light, beckoning her, and heard beautiful music. The angel took her hand. My aunt would have gone with her except that her mother, my grandmother (despite the fact she was thousands of miles away) appeared in the vision as well. She took her other hand, and urgently called her back.

That's when my aunt woke up.

This released a whole stream of angel stories. We talked about angels all through dinner. My daughter listened wide-eyed as we told stories about angels appearing in strange circumstances, protecting people. Finally, reverently, as if they were in the room with us, she said the names of two victims of a serial killer. "And where," she asked softly, "was the angel for them?"

I don't know why angels seem to appear

sometimes and not others. I've heard enough stories about interventions to believe they happen. Even when it seems they don't. I believe the power of goodness is stronger than the power of evil, and God's compassion for the vulnerable to be beyond measure.

Such anguish goes beyond any attempt at theological explanation. We have only the steady assurance that God's universe is larger than death.

May 8: **Personality type**

I once worked on a committee with a whole group of people who were "intuitives." Intuitive types make decisions by leaps instead of logical thought. If someone asks how they figured something out, they say it was a hunch. Furthermore, they're not keen on little details like what time it is, and how long will this take. Being tuned mainly inward does that.

That committee was an adventure in creativity, with the one person who wasn't an intuitive type carrying a great burden of detail. She finally rebelled and demanded someone else start keeping track of the time, and figuring out who was going to do what, when.

But no one got mad at anyone else, not even her. It's great to have personality theories to objectify why people act the way they do.

May 9: **Pottery**

Wherever I go, I return with local pottery, made from local clay. A mug, if I have little money, a jug or bowl if I have more. The potter's art fills me with awe.

I am amazed at this ability to take earth and bake it into something lovely. I take this local piece of earth home. No caravaner, carrying the art of Phoenicia along the trading routes of history, could be prouder than me climbing onto a plane clutching my fragile cups or bowls.

What wonder, that pieces of the Mother Earth can give delight halfway round the world.

May 10: **Solidarity**

I met Mirtala in a church in El Salvador. She had

been picked up by the police for her work with an organization that was helping Salvadoran refugees return home. As our interpreter repeated her words in English, she told the story of her torture. I wrote, unable to weep, needing to tell her story.

Mirtala was one of the lucky ones, alive and on her way to see a doctor. A few weeks later, she was back on the border, accompanying returning refugees. Soon after that, the civil war exploded. Six Jesuit priests and their housekeeper and their housekeeper's daughter were murdered. Mirtala was missing. The brave minister of the church where we had met her was in jail.

I was back in Canada by then. I told her story everywhere I could. When other women heard the story of her agony, they pressured their own government to intervene. Who knows what effect it had; but they knew another woman's pain as their own.

That's what solidarity is. We feel another's pain as our own.

May 11: **Mirtala in El Salvador**

The Americans are weeping
even Jennifer, interpreting like a mirror
atonement
they are paying
for being *gringos*

Already words form in my mind
let them feel the bite of handcuffs,
the blindfolded shove down endless stairs
let them smell the harsh chemical
the warm liquid on your breasts

The orders
ten names or we will will cut them off and
the thin rope around your nipples
lifting until you faint.

The air is hot and liquid and we breathe your
memories
through our mouths

We breathe in your geometry of despair,
angled walls, straight rope,

five-cornered shadow of your fear
and in the middle, a demon
where men once stood.

May 12: **Respect**

Re-spect means to look again. Most of our ways of seeing benefit from a long looking again. First Nations people call us to live with respect in Creation, looking again at the world the Creator gave us.

And ourselves. Analyst James Hillman has said dreams are simply trying to persuade us to re-spect ourselves, to look again at forgotten childhood.

And women. There's this long passage in the Book of Proverbs that has always given me trouble. It describes the virtuous wife, and how she spins and weaves and buys land and rises while it is yet dark to feed her family – an impossible ideal that makes me feel tired. But there is this verse I hadn't noticed. "She is strong and respected and not afraid of the future," the writer says.

My trouble with this passage was that I thought her work was taken for granted. But it wasn't. She was respected. Looking back is always worth the trouble.

May 13: **Forgiveness**

It's easy to become enmeshed in the profound dilemmas of forgiveness. What about apologies, repentance, never-doing-this-again? Should people in exploitative relationships, just keep fogiving, seventy times seven, as Jesus said?

Foster Freed, a wise pastor I often consult, says that "forgiveness is impossible, until we see it is not optional." It's helpful, he says, that Jesus gives these statements in the form of a command.

Being a follower of this Jesus person is not easy. Sometimes I act as if it is. I forget that this Jewish peasant came with an agenda so radical and different from the way people normally behave, that it's impossible. And we have nothing left but grace, God's steadfast and forgiving love.

May 14: **Forgiveness prayer**

Grace is undeserved forgiveness, undeserved love, the fruits of a generous heart that asks nothing in return. It comes from God. Sometimes humans can attempt it.

Forgiveness Prayer

Loving God,
When I am feeling vengeful, remind me of your grace.
When I get tired of trying to figure out what is right, remind me of your grace.
Help me seek justice, and remind me of your grace.
Help me be loving, and remind me of your grace and love.
Amen

May 15: **Fairness**

Once, talking and mostly listening, to a friend on the phone, my middle child suddenly appeared cheerfully offering a much-thumbed book by Scott Peck, ready for use at the appropriate page. Just where I frequently quoted it to him. "Life is difficult," says Peck. "This is a great truth, one of the greatest truths."

Women do housework and mind the babies and have careers and try to make things work. We must watch where we travel after dark. If we enter a non-traditional profession, we have to be tough, God help us if we have an attack of the weeps in the boardroom.

It's not fair. Peck is right, life is difficult. We just make ourselves unhappy by expecting it to be otherwise. So we need to fight our battles. But we also need to come to terms with the built-in unfairness of everyone's life, and enjoy ourselves in the middle of it. Or we will go mad, wishing.

May 16: **Friends**

Lack of self-worth traps us in different ways. I have trouble initiating contact with old friends. I am too tired at the end of the day, my work is intense, I don't want any more time on the phone.

But the truth is, I can't imagine why I would be valuable to anyone, why anyone would look forward to my call. Despite this, I am blessed with friends who seek me out. They won't let me isolate myself because of this peculiar sense of worthlessness, carried only in the heart. My mind knows I am perfectly acceptable.

I am not alone in this. Even if we don't feel worthy, we need to acknowledge that we are. We are made in God's image.

May 17: **Aging**

A friend loves to describe the day she knew when she had reached middle age. She went into a store and looked at clothes for some time with the attentive and thoughtful assistance of the young woman who worked there. "I'm just going to go out to my car to get the blouse I'm trying to match," she said finally, "and I'll be right back."

She came right back, and presented herself, blouse in hand, to the same saleswoman, who looked at her without a shred of recognition. "Yes, ma'am, is there anything I can help you with today?" she asked politely.

Women become invisible at a certain age.

There is nothing we can do about this. Except enjoy our invisibility (shoplifting is not a viable option) and surprise people sometimes by speaking loudly from where they are sure there is no living creature. The Raging Grannies, who startle onlookers by singing outrageous songs about peace and justice, have built a whole movement around this principle.

No matter how young we are, it's a good idea to plan for the day when we can no longer be seen by the naked eye.

May 18: **Failure**

Mostly I deal with failure by denying it as much as possible. Sometimes, though, when I'm feeling very brave, I peek inside and let myself see the workshop that went badly, the book that didn't sell, the relationship that died, the money (such a visible sign of failure) unearned.

Then I shut that door as fast as I can.

I know something dark lurks behind it by the days when I can read neither the best-seller list or my bank balance. Counting successes does nothing to help. For perfectionist women, any blot mars the whole.

The head cannot help in this at all. My head knows the workshop failed because I took a risk and tried something new; the relationship failed because we are – after all – human; the bank balance is low because I chose to follow my passion. But that does no good. Only our dreams and our friends, both of whom speak the language of the heart, can save us.

Success is knowing how to love unconditionally our friends and our own self. Both. All else is failure in disguise.

May 19: **Stress**

After many years of placing myself in new situations (journalists do this, it's our job) and feeling awkward and tense, I've figured out a useful truth. No new situation is as stressful the second day. It's not as new anymore, and much stress comes from newness.

It took a long time to come to this conclusion. One way of coping when our mind and body decides it's in a crisis is to regress toward childhood. From that immature point of view, I couldn't generalize enough to see that I had felt this way before, and the feeling always receded.

I'm writing this down so I don't forget.

Women are enormously adaptable. That biology will get us through.

May 20: **Money**

Few things propel women faster backward into childhood, than money. For some, in what sociologists call the "family of origin," money was a source of wrangling. In order not to duplicate that, we refuse to discuss money at all. Denial is the operative word.

Others saw money used as a weapon to keep our mothers subservient. We are filled with diffuse anger about that, and a fierce desire to be absolutely independent financially.

Others had families with plenty of money, but it was still a source of lecturing, withholding, or bribing – none of them healthy activities. Others are the survivors of deep poverty, and carry the marks common to survivors: never-ending guilt, never-ending responsibility.

Our desire for consumer goods is human, not immoral. But when we are overwhelmed by imagined needs, it's good to ask what we are seeking: money, or a happy childhood.

May 21: **Belief**

People sometimes say in wonder, "You believe in dreams. Why is that?" They seldom say (but most accept) that I believe in God, the Bible, Jesus, angels. I do, after all, go to church.

This is strange. The dreams are there. How can I not believe in a reality that presents itself to me night after night?

It's the same with the Bible. It is there. It is a book of mighty stories that teach me more than I can ever learn. It is solid and flawed, full of ambiguity and cruelty and wisdom. A reality. I cannot make it go away, any more than a Moslem woman could make the Koran go away.

I have seen Jesus in the manger in 50 Christmas pageants. He has been black, white, male, female. Real. God has spoken in my dreams, a reality I can neither conjure nor destroy.

And every week or so, an angel appears on my doorstep, says "Are you free for lunch tomorrow? I need to talk." She says, "You're working too hard, here's supper." She hands me a casserole that will last for three days. I don't have to believe in her, I just say thank you.

Belief cannot be forced. There are realities we accept or not.

May 22: **Loneliness**

If women are to be creative, we must be lonely sometimes. And solitude, like all good things, like fire, water, sun, rain, has a destructive side.

When the silence grows too strong and wants to have us all to itself, day after day; when the creative work takes all our energy and leaves us nothing to meet with others; if we are lucky, our friends will come and rescue us. Not too soon, or our painting, writing, singing, thinking will go undone. And not too late, or we will lose our soul.

We should never underestimate the power of solitude for good and ill.

May 23: **Ambiguity**

I distrust anyone who is sure of the answers. Even when I agree with them, a view of the world that sees no grey makes me nervous.

This probably comes from doing a lot of dream work, from knowing that just around the corner of every inner symbol and imagined truth, there is another truth, another insight, seen from a different angle. And that changes the whole thing.

This world is seldom clean and sure. The ability to suffer ambiguity makes it easier to live in it.

May 24: **Hope**

It's planting time. I have carried seedlings in and

out at night until they are hardy enough to live out on their own.

I have discovered again how good it is for women to garden. There are things we learned as toddlers, handing seed potatoes to our grandmothers or grandfathers: that our strength comes from the land and we are nothing when we are separated from it; that it is our mother indeed.

Jesus knew this, as the child of rural people. He knew if he spoke of the power in a tiny mustard seed, his listeners would instinctively understand the potential he described. He knew the phrase "lilies of the field" would evoke overwhelming loveliness, and his audience would rejoice in the love of a Creator who offers rain and sun for their delight.

Even the tiniest garden, even a pot of geraniums on a windowsill, is full of hope.

May 25: **Passions**

About the end of May a small passion – a disease, really – overtakes our neighborhood. In my case it eventually spirals downward into madness.

Gardening. I get up with the sun, a little earlier each day, and rush outside in the grip of delirium. I cover and uncover seedlings, ritualistically.

I take foolish risks. I plant them out too early. Other gardeners assemble and we confer with much shaking of heads, like a doctor hovering over a bedside. "It's too soon," we assure each other. As soon as they leave I rush to the back yard and plant more, guilt-ridden, feverish, addicted.

Because of this, I understand, without always condoning, certain sins that have their origin in desire. When chastened men tell me (as they do at times – I'm what you call a good listener) how their marriage collapsed in pursuit of another woman, I nod. I understand lust precisely. It's the feeling I have for my spouse 11 months of the year, and each May, for the greenhouse I cannot yet afford.

People who lust after glass houses shouldn't throw stones.

May 26: **Suffering**

God does not send suffering as a way of strengthening us, or testing us, or making sure we will look forward to heaven. God does not send suffering at all. God is simply with us when we are in pain.

Suffering is not written into our lives when we are born. We are not fated to suffer. If we can find nothing to thank God for in the midst of pain, God will not be angry.

Suffering is not noble. It is appropriate to rage and scream at God when we are in pain; God will not be antagonized by this. The only crack of light in this matter of suffering is the peculiar intimacy it brings with others who suffer too, and who stand beside you and offer you their tears without denying their own pain.

Look closely. Theirs is the face of God.

May 27: **Holy Writing**

The Bible, the Koran, the Talmud, all the sacred texts speak to us at unconscious levels. We may think we are approaching the stories rationally.

But their real power is that the stories awaken certain characters within ourselves.

A friend of mine once did an advent study by taking the characters of the story and trying to find them inside himself. Where in me is the pure place, like Mary, fit for God to be born? he asked. Where in me is the simplicity of the shepherds?

He discovered, he says, that he couldn't find those characters until he first found Herod. Once he found the angry tyrant within, the part of himself that is threatened by new life, the space opened up.

Not a very literal reading of the sacred text, he admits. He reads it as living word, something you encounter, something different every time.

Whatever our Holy Book, we need to go fearlessly into it.

May 28: **Poems**

It is extremely important to write poetry. No poetry that honestly undertakes to capture some particularity of life is bad. The very effort is a poem. It makes us look at life.

Poems are written about things we see and feel; so when we write one, we stop and look and feel.

This honors our Creator, who made all pain and joy, all beauty, the heart of all our poems. God cares little about fashions of rhyme and meter. God loves the held breath, the wonder, the stretch to say what we mean.

Our words won't be right. Never mind. We leave perfection to God, whose business it is. *Our* business is to notice God's business.

May 29: **Regret**

My middle child, the swimmer, offers advice to his younger sister. She is trapped in a decision-making paradox, paralyzed.

Sometimes you just have to make a decision, he tells her, and neither is completely the right one or the wrong one. You just have to go ahead and take one of them, and *don't look back*. It is the swimmer's creed.

Regret is seldom a useful emotion. Paths not taken are soon consumed by the jungle of daily life. *Don't look back.*

Whatever we regret not doing – or doing – we can lament and then go on. Otherwise we drown.

May 30: **Rituals**

When my daughter was 16 she came to me calmly and told me she was going to get drunk that night at a party, and I shouldn't worry.

I was unhappy. I fear the mix of youth and booze greatly, and said so. "We're watching out for each other," she said confidently, "at the party. And we have a designated driver."

I honored her confidence. We talked for awhile – mostly me talking, telling her every worry I had. She listened attentively and then she went, drank beer, and came home with three friends. She was very sick. I was deeply unhappy.

When she felt better that afternoon, she phoned each of her friends, except those who had been there, and told them all about the party.

That's when I realized that getting drunk is a peculiar, toxic ritual of growing up. She needs to mark the change to adulthood and separation from her parents. Like other coming-of-age rituals in other cultures, this one involves both danger and an altered state of consciousness. Her confirmation – not being noted by most of her peers nor sufficiently separate from her church-going parents – is not enough.

Rituals stamp the awareness of a change into the vision of onlookers so they cannot forget; that is their purpose. Some are more painful than others.

May 31: **Accompaniment**

The essence of friendship can be found in the extraordinary work of some people in Montreal (and other cities, too, it's just that this is where I observed them).

They accompany people seeking refugee status to the hearings that will decide whether or not they can stay in Canada. They don't do the legal work. They just go with them at a scary time.

This is what happens in a friendship. We

JUNE

June 1: **Consumerism**

We live in a society which won't be able to provide all the goodies advertised on television for all its children.

So we'd better raise children who are happy with themselves as creative beings, not as little consumers. They'd better be valued for what they are – loving, building, drawing, sculpting, singing, cooking children of God – not for what they can buy. Valued for their own creative selves.

It wouldn't hurt to get down on the floor

and build a block tower with a three-year-old just as soon as possible.

June 2: **Solitude**

When we first moved into a neighborhood I was nervous. What if it was really the way it seemed on television – women popping in for coffee every hour or so?

Not that I dislike coffee, or visiting. Both are essential, especially the talking. Especially with a loved friend. But equally essential is solitary time for reading or writing down a dream or thinking about it.

That's not easy to explain. It's fine to say you're working or painting or gardening. But try suggesting you plan to spend the day – well – thinking.

As it turned out, the other women in the neighborhood weren't at all as television suggested. They all had jobs. So while a ten a.m. coffee break may have been in order, it wasn't taking place in my kitchen. I had my time to empty myself, to still the inner chatter, to be quiet enough – as theologian Henri Nouwen said – to be able to hear others, and be truly hospitable.

Contrary to popular belief, solitude is not an illness; it is a cure.

June 3: **Death**

We are more in charge of the timetable of our lives than we know. For instance. My mother, now in her 80s, dreamed that my father (who died some years ago) appeared in front of her with a suitcase. "Time to go," he said cheerfully.

"I'm not ready yet," she said, equally cheerfully.

My mother had decided not to die.

"We'll have no more dreams about dying, Grandma." said her granddaughter firmly when she heard about this. (She has learned from her grandma to be blunt.)

My mother laughed. We know what keeps her here.

A woman's "no" is a powerful statement, especially when propelled by love.

June 4: **Hanging clothes**

I love hanging out laundry. As Thomas Moore, the monk turned author, says, there is an enchantment in everyday things.

Every sense, including memory, comes alive. The soft wind and the sun touch my skin. I can see my mother, younger, standing in our back porch with clothespins in her mouth. I can see my father (unusual for those days) reeling in the line when rain threatened, folding the clothes carefully in the basket.

Angels in the ordinary. Oh, mostly I am too busy to do anything but whip the clothes from washer to dryer. And anyhow, we're so liberated in this house everyone does their own laundry, and have since they were eight.

But once in a while, I slip into the past and visit my young mother and hang out the clothes, and they come in sundried and smelling like childhood. And I am not rushed.

Our past, if we let it talk to us, can critique our present.

June 5: **Family history**

My children tell me this. When they were little they sometimes arrived home from school to see our coffee pot, smoke-blackened, sitting in the snow outside the kitchen door. This pleased them.

They knew this is what it meant: Mom's writing is going well. She has forgotten the coffee on the stove. She put it on to occupy her hands while she untangled a thought and, some time later – the coffee having boiled dry while she wrote – threw the smoking pot out the kitchen door.

The house would smell bitter when they entered. To this day, they say, the acrid smell of burnt coffee makes them happy. All is well with the world, this smell says.

When they are little, we are the center of our children's lives. And all they ask is that we be happy.

June 6: **Personality type**

Sometimes my husband and I work together to do a seminar or project. He makes it wonderfully fun; he's relaxed and funny and full of ideas.

We differ, though, in a crucial way. He likes to keep all his (our, in this case) options open. And I like to get things all sewed up. Early.

This could lead to a certain amount of tension. However, we've been friends for a long time, and we've stopped (mostly) regarding the other as crazy. It's just the way we are made, just the way we approach life.

So I try to trust that he really does have a plan, under all that ruminating about how "we could do this," or "we could do that," and "had you thought of..." For his part, he tries to come down to some decisions knowing I will be restless until we do.

It's taken time.

When someone we love drives us crazy, unwittingly, it's likely a personality difference. Not their fault, and not ours.

June 7: **Friends**

It's possible for men and women, even married to other people, to be friends. Very carefully. Even across the demilitarized zone of gender warfare and despite the hazards of mutual attraction and the potential for gossip.

There are rules:

1. Lunch is less likely to attract gossip than dinner.
2. A common task, a businesslike notebook open on the table, makes inquisitive onlookers feel better.
3. The marriages of both need to be in excellent shape, or the nature of the friendship can metamorphose rapidly.
4. The spouses of both need to be unthreatened by the friendship.

Such friendships are worthwhile because men and women need the way each other think. We have so much in common as a species, and we are so alien to one another. Absorbing each other's peculiar ways in conversation we become wiser, more conscious, and more complete.

Only foolish women disregard the wisdom of men.

June 8: **Authority**

There's an interesting picture of women's authority in the story of Joanna, Mary, and Mary the mother of James going to the tomb after Jesus is killed, to anoint the body. It couldn't have been easy. They had authority, though; women's authority to deal with matters of death and the body, as well as the raw courage to risk being branded subversive.

When, instead of the body, the women find two angels who inform them Jesus has "been raised," they return from the tomb and tell the other followers of Jesus.

The others don't believe them.

Peter, in fact, goes to look for himself. And later, when Paul tells the story, the women are omitted completely, despite their courage. Peter becomes the one who announces the risen Christ.

This story is enough to make every woman who has ever had to squirrel some resolution through a meeting by getting a guy to lend approval to it grind her teeth.

And every woman who has spent a good part of her time changing diapers knows that attending to matters of the body is not a task to be taken lightly.

Now the biblical record is being looked at with a critical eye. Mary and Joanna and Mary the mother of James (spare a thought for her identity struggle) are being granted their due.

The courage to do the dirty work carries within it the authority to bear witness.

June 9: **Wise old women**

I have a wonderful elderly woman friend who tells me what she thinks. We talk to each other in a way my peers, age-wise, don't. We might work on a dream together and she'll tell me gently but quite firmly that it seems to be indicating I'm too rigid. Or whatever.

This is not done. She does it anyway, and I love her dearly for it. She has earned the right to throw away the rules: she is old and wise and has suffered much. She has known me for many years, and loves me in spite of the rather large amount of my personal shadow she has seen. And her intuition, at her age, is so finely honed I trust it.

She is a wise old woman.

I aspire to be like her.

June 10: **Photographs**

My mother has come for dinner, laden with boxes of old black and white photographs. "I can't really see them anyway," she says cheerfully. "I think you should have them here." Her grandchildren sit around the table, shuffling through them. Here is one of her and my father, achingly young. She looks up at him smiling, while he regards her with the awed tenderness peculiar to the newly married. Here is another, years later; she is laughing in the sun while my brother and I play with a puppy on the dock.

The photographs unleash a flood of memories; like the day, as a young bride, she filled the wood stove in their little, neat apartment chock-full, and lit it. This started a chimney fire whose manic roaring could be heard throughout the building. We laugh at the eager innocence with which she tells the story. She and my daughter seem almost the same age – young, full of wonder at the duplicity of her own stove betraying an unsuspecting housewife.

Chronos time describes how we grow old. Kairos time – when it is clear the universe is filled with love – describes how we live at certain rare moments.

June 11: **Indispensability**

In order to do certain creative things – writing, praying, mothering, teaching, things like that – you have to believe the world is waiting for this, hoping. You can never ever believe your work might not be needed. Dispensable. It's the understanding that the world is waiting, breathless, for what you are producing that drives the creative force.

On the other hand, as soon as we begin to feel we are truly indispensable, we do bizarre things. We refuse to take time off work, even when we are exhausted. We stop delegating. At home, indispensability can look a lot like territoriality, in which no one can manage the kitchen the way we do, no one can serve up quite such nutritious meals.

Even as I write this, I am emerging from just such a period. What I had to do, I felt, no one else could do, and furthermore, it had to be done by a certain date. When I hit a wall (too many early mornings and late nights working) I was persuaded by loving friends to renegotiate the deadline. I had to give up the immediate notion of indispensability, the mask (one of my favorite) of invincibility.

I came out of my office and realized I had been absent in my own home. The fridge was full of odd, rotting things.

No one is truly indispensable. Often, however, we are much loved and valuable.

June 12: **Manipulation**

People without power become extraordinarily skilled at arranging things to suit themselves without others seeing it. Manipulation: the small sentence uttered in public that cries out "poor me, my spouse, my children pay no attention to me... "; or the skillful arranging of seeming options until the victim is trapped into doing what the manipulator wishes. Children, especially when parents are busy, become expert at moving from one parent to another and saying "He promised..." and "she promised..."

All this is understandable. Women who lack power can become consummate manipulators, working beneath the surface to get what they need.

We can forgive ourselves for this, when we do it. We've learned it from our ancestors; we've often needed it to survive. But when we have power – and many of us do, now – there is no excuse for not being aboveboard.

Working beneath the surface is a tool only for those who have no power.

June 13: **Creativity**

It looks like selfishness, and sometimes it may be. But protecting our own creative time for reflection or art or meditation or thinking or praying is a necessary selfishness. We can't rest ourselves, or heal ourselves, or hear the universe speak to us without it.

Women have an absolute right to their own time.

June 14: **Truth-telling**

It's hard for women to tell the unvarnished truth. Often, the truth hurts and our mothers reminded us, after all, that "if you can't say something good about someone, don't say anything at all."

But I know of a high-school teacher who sexually abused the most vulnerable of his young women students for 20 years. Some parents suspected this, and warned away their daughters. The man wasn't stopped from seeking out others with unerring instinct, until – when the school hired a woman principal – a few students felt confident enough to approach her.

Discerning and speaking the truth in any situation is not easy. But it's part of being adult.

June 15: **Rituals**

When children are little, they want fabulous birthday cakes shaped like trains. I can't do this. It always comes out either round or square, graced by my meek effort to write their name on it and a lot of Smarties®.

This failing is now lost in the mists of time. Making the cake is a ritual to indulge in if now-grown offspring happen to be home within a month or two, either way, of a birthday. Mixing, thinking of these beloved people, hiding it until the right moment are moments of memory-filled pleasure.

And then the last of the ritual: the lights turned off so the room is in darkness; the youngest person present carrying in the cake, blazing; the singing, the blowing out of candles. The long storytelling. "I remember the night you were born..."; and "I remember the year you were five..."

We know these stories by heart. But without these marks of ritual – fire, song, repetition, candles, quiet reflection, narrative, memory, movement, gesture – our lives would come unstitched.

Making a birthday cake is a sacred task, even if it isn't train-shaped.

June 16: **Birthday Cake (Chocolate)**

Stir: 1/2 cup boiling water and 3 squares of unsweetened chocolate until thick.

Cream: 1/2 cup shortening, 1 2/3 cups sugar and 3 eggs, with the above chocolate mixture, and beat for five minutes.

Blend: 2 1/4 cups cake flour, 2 1/4 tsps baking powder, 1/4 tsp baking soda, 1 tsp salt.

Mix into the creamed mixture alternately with 1 cup buttermilk, just until smooth. Bake in two greased and floured pans, 8" or 9" x 1 1/2" , at 350°F for 30 to 40 minutes. (It's done when no imprint remains when you touch it lightly with your finger.)

Ice with chocolate icing: Blend 1/3 cup soft butter, 3 cups icing sugar, about 3 tbsp milk or strong coffee, 1 1/2 tsp vanilla. Add 3 squares unsweetened melted chocolate.

June 17: **Birthday Cake (White)**

Combine: 2 1/4 cups cake flour, 2 1/2 tsp baking powder,
1/2 tsp salt

Cream: 1 1/4 cups sugar, 1/2 cup butter

Combine: 1 cup milk, 1 tsp vanilla

Mix: dry ingredients and liquids, alternately, one-third at a time, with the creamed ingredients. Stir until smooth with each addition.

Whip: 4 large egg whites until stiff, but not dry, and fold into batter.

Bake: in layers at 350°F for about 25 minutes. (It's done when no imprint remains when you touch it lightly with your finger.)

Ice: with any lemon, orange, or chocolate icing. (You could use the icing recipe on page 158: omit the chocolate and substitute lemon or orange juice for the milk, vanilla and coffee.)

June 18: **Marriage**

When I was married, I believed the definition of "husband" was as follows: male person who builds shelves and fixes things, moving unobtrusively around the house to set things right. I am sure he had an equally firm definition of "wife."

It has taken me years to come to terms with the mistakenness of my belief.

Marriage is an exercise in accepting another person for who he or she is, in loving unconditionally. Both partners need to pull their weight; but perception is a wily beast. Sometimes each of you feel you are doing 75% of the work.

So we buy our shelves. I fix faulty doorknobs and broken chairs. He rakes lawns and mows. We both laugh (me hysterically) at his deep love for changing lightbulbs. It's a household skill he manages well.

The other day he got up on our very steep, very high roof to see where it was leaking while I held the ladder and promised God that if this wonderful man got safely down again, this wise and gentle man who solves crises and makes me laugh, I would never again complain.

My definition of "husband" has broadened considerably.

Marriage is like any other friendship. It

is about loving your self and loving the other, unconditionally.

June 19: **The Enneagram**

God has nine faces.
They say women have two.
That makes us two-ninths the size of God.

So here I am, looking out with God's eyes,
two of them,
on the world.
Got to get this place cleaned up!
No wait, that's not God talking
that's me.

Try again.
Here, world, try it this way!
No, that's still take-charge me, talking...
What would God do?
God would weep.

June 20: **Soul**

The world is coming alive again, bit by bit. For too long, theologians have fooled us into thinking that trees don't have souls, dogs don't have souls. Scholars in the Middle Ages asked *Habet mulier animam?* Do women have souls? Most scholars now are over that.

When the soul of the world has been repressed for a long time, it rises in unfamiliar ways. People who have even a dim instinct that trees have a form of consciousness go out and hug them so they won't be cut down. This would be an entirely uncomplicated activity except that loggers also have souls.

People ascribe healing powers to crystals, sensing there is life in stones. There is vibrational medicine, subtle energies, holograms. We are praying for people hundreds of miles away and sending messages of loving intentionality to plants.

Strong animals appear in our dreams.

All this because we cannot live in a universe without a soul. Just in time, we have noticed the earth is alive.

June 21: **Shadows**

Most women are able now, to recognize when they are projecting outward some of their own, dark, inner material. When I become annoyed, for example, at someone who rushes past me and dismisses me, I recognize my own tendency to be too busy.

But we seldom recognize how we project outward our goodness, our white shadow. We put some people – generous volunteers, caring pastors, well-rounded doctors – on pedestals, regarding them as saints and heroes. We push husbands in certain directions in their careers instead of following up those interests and pursuing them ourselves.

Hyperadmiration springs from our own soul, our own ability to be generous and gentle and wise; we need to live out those good qualities ourselves. Asking, or allowing, someone else to live out our good instincts is as dangerous as letting others live out our darkness.

June 22: **Creation**

There are two different stories of how my spouse and I met. We handle this the same way the authors of Genesis handle their conflicting stories. We put the two versions of the creation of our relationship side-by side. Each is important. We can't remember which came first and they are now mythic, spun into a tale we tell our children about the origin of their species.

Most couples do this. Having a creation myth is a way of declaring that this narrative is sacred. And the very nature of the myth announces what precisely is most precious and unassailable in the marriage.

We met the night Kennedy was shot. That established a certain dramatic tone, a passion for global politics in our marriage. We also met (the other version) giggling in Anthropology class. We produce that myth when we are mutually feeling young and light-headed, as antidote to the blood and tragedy of the other.

Each holy union contains its own myth which begins the story of the tribe.

June 23: **Order**

There is something mystical about the hardware store; all that shelving, all those bins and boxes are chanting a hymn to the principle of order. Walking down those aisles is an adventure in promise; chaos can be defeated and lives brought under control.

We humans yearn for order. Sometimes it even happens for awhile. But then it slips away, nudged out of sight by the gods who like humans to be always a little off-balance, always a little creative, never stagnant.

Experts talk about the end of history. If we ever really did get every room in the house clean at the same time, *that* would be the end of history.

June 24: **Sarai**

One trouble many of us have with the Bible is the way its women seem so flawed. Poor barren Sarai, for example, offering her slave Hagar to her husband. "Perhaps she can have a child for me," she says. Then, overcome by her own competitive nature and Hagar's sudden pride, she is so cruel the surrogate mother has to flee. (Gen. 16:1–6)

We could explain this as a story written by patriarchal men who disliked women. Unfortunately, the man in this picture comes off no better. Abram, the husband, suggests to the angry Sarai that she do what she likes with the woman who is, after all, carrying his child.

But we could also look for the Sarai in ourselves. The story wouldn't have lasted all these years unless Sarai's behavior spoke for the times we ourselves have felt barren of creativity and power and asked someone else – our husbands, our children, a politician, a film star we admire – to carry those elements for us, to be rich or famous or skilled or perfect on our behalf. And when they cannot be the saints we ask, we grow embittered.

It's easy to imagine the Mary, the one full of expectation, within us. But when we reach out to the barren and bitter Sarai within, she can weep at last.

June 25: **Decisions**

Some good friends were thinking of buying an old house and they couldn't decide what to do.

Many of their friends went through the house, several times, looking, reflecting. We all came to know a lot about the house; in fact, we all fell in love with it, and with the idea of them in it. We began to see birthday parties in it, and visiting at Christmas, and sitting in the big old kitchen having coffee...

Ultimately they made the decision. They moved in awhile ago, and they indeed love the house. It fits them like a glove. "What I learned in this," says my friend happily, "is always to consult your friends when you're trying to make a decision."

There are worse ways to make choices than to consult someone who knows us well. They decided for themselves, of course. But they also could trust the fact they were well-loved – enough that had they been utterly carried away by some folly, these companions would have made small murmurs of despair.

We get by with a little help from our friends.

June 26: **Father**

My father loved to garden. He's dead now, but always with me, planting cosmos or nasturtiums, offering advice. I suppose you could say I have a ghost. Or an angel.

A strange woman, you're probably thinking. Why does she go on about someone who lived in the past? But women need an antidote to our culture's inability to conceive of anything other than the present. The world around us has little loyalty to the past, and less to the future.

That's wrong. We women carry the future inside us. At some level we know that. We know there is continuity between the generations, past and future, backward and forward. Native elders teach us we are responsible for seven generations.

So in the garden, I talk to my father. And my great-great-grandchildren, too. They're not here either, but that doesn't bother me. I am looking after the soil, I assure them, no pesticides at all.

And they are pleased.

June 27: **Inner Discipline**

Women, as a species, are subject to the most iron-firm inner policing. A friend of mine who is a fine writer always finds it hard to sit and write or read (the two go together) because of a family prohibition in her childhood against "wasting time." Girls reading books were wasting time, and there was always plenty to do.

Now she must defeat that regulation every time she sits down to write, quietly telling her "inner police" (which is how this aspect of ourselves appears in dreams) to go elsewhere.

Meditating on what was forbidden in our childhood can often show us what militates against our creativity today. And then we can tell that particular officer to go away.

June 28: **Goddesses**

Analyst and author James Hillman says the problem with Christianity is that it has only one God, one story, and that can't quite account for the full range of human behavior. "What we now call the unconscious are the old gods returning, assaulting," he says, "climbing over the walls of the ego."

I like what he says very much, even as I stay safely within the walls of my faith. And Christianity is beginning to discover its other stories. Instead of one story of suffering, death and resurrection, now we find stories of exile and exodus and birth and survival. We are discovering there is more than Yahweh, there is a woman-Goddess, a Mother-God, who gives birth to us and gathers us to her. Some of us look at Eve and see, not sin, but the courage to grow up.

June 29: **Identity**

Some ways of being woman are learned. We ignore the possibilities of our daughters' careful observation of us at our peril. A story about our youngest, born when I was well into my work as a writer.

She was maybe a year and a half old – in that charming preverbal stage when children chatter constantly in highly inflected syllables that make no sense. Every day she spent a lot of time "talking" on her little red plastic phone. One day, curious, I sat and listened. All her strings of garbled sounds ended on an interrogative note, followed by short affirmative murmurings. Her phone was tucked into her right shoulder and she was making rapid pencil scratches on a piece of paper as she muttered.

She was interviewing someone. She couldn't talk yet but she was doing what Mommy did.

We mothers need to be conscious of our selves. The way we are, and what we do, is locked away in a box (along with other things from other loved people) in our daughters' souls. Every day they pick and choose from it as they decide who they will be.

June 30: **Prayer**

Loving God
I ask today for eyes to see the beauty in your world's soul.
I ask today for strength to bear the pain in its depths.

JULY

July 1: **Gaia's temperature**

There are several ways to check the health of the planet. One can watch the news on television.

Or one can go outside, garden for awhile, and watch the birds.

One can walk by water, listen for loons, and feed the ducks.

One can paddle a canoe into a bog and see how many frogs there are.

The most important news isn't always found on television.

July 2: **About roses**

I keep roses on the table
as antidote.

I let the words come out more now
I tell them
What I think about the forest
And what they do in it.
And sometime you know (when the children are grown)
I'll lie down in front of trucks
not bloodied at all
when they cruise over me
because I'm immune.

I have roses.

July 3: **Grandmothers**

My father's mother emigrated from England. She had long black hair and lived alone in a tiny house with a big verandah in a mining town. When I stayed with my grandmother she made chips (the English term) deepfried in lots of dangerous hot fat. She made kites and paper flowers and played the piano by ear.

In the mornings, I would climb into bed with her and we would have tea with lots of milk, and talk. I would comb her long hair.

From her I learned that grandmothers are beautiful and young (in a grandaughter's eyes) and love their grandchildren unconditionally. They spend time with grandchildren and seldom have rules, although they may offer wise advice. They have lived longer than the rest of us, in more places, and have a wider view. A few of them remember how it was before television.

Many of us will be grandmothers. We need to equip ourselves with wisdom for that day.

July 4: **Scones**

My grandmother made scones as well as kites. This was her favorite recipe. Any occasion which requires that you endear yourself to an elderly person from "the old country" can be greatly improved with these, served hot with butter and marmalade or honey.

2 cups flour
3 tsp baking powder
1/2 tsp baking soda (generous)
1/2 tsp salt
6 large tbsp sugar
3 1/2 tbsp shortening
1 egg
1 cup raisins
3/4 cup buttermilk
1 tsp lemon flavoring

Mix dry ingredients together. Rub in shortening as you would for pastry. Add raisins. Add well-beaten eggs and milk. Mix together. Pat out to a circle 1/2 inch thick and cut into scones (as if you were cutting a pie into eight pieces.) Bake at 450°F for 10 min.

July 5: **Death**

Dreaming about someone dying doesn't always mean that's what's going to happen. When a dream wants to talk about actual death, it's more subtle. (It's not a bad idea to check out their travel plans, though, just in case.) So a dream of a parent dying might mean some parental quality is giving way to make room for something else, maybe something more suited to our grown-up personality.

A dream of anyone dying should evoke two questions: "What qualities do I associate with this person?" and "Are these qualities disappearing in me?"

Women live so much with the expectations of others that when we stop doing that and start living by our own creed it is a kind of death. But a necessary one.

In our inner life, as in the outer world, nothing lives forever. Some things have to be given up before we can grow.

July 6: **Table discussions**

There is something about sitting around a table that induces frank discussion. Especially the breakfast table. Maybe there's something about wearing pyjamas that prevents pride and defensiveness from interfering with the conversation.

Once a small group of young women arrived to sleep at our house after a party. They had had something stronger than cola to drink. In the morning, I mixed up biscuits, their favorite, and called them to breakfast.

"I won't tell on you," I said (avoiding looking at my own daughter.) "But I won't lie to your parents for you either. I don't like this. Please don't make this house the one you collapse into after a drinking party."

We munched on biscuits smeared variously with marmalade or strawberry jam, drank orange juice, talked about parties in my day, and parties in theirs, and the nature of life for young women today. There's a lot more booze now, I suggested, and more drugs. The stakes are higher around unprotected sex – from the risk of an unwanted pregnancy to the risk of a death sentence. It's very hard being a young woman today.

"We look after each other," one of them said proudly. There were murmurs of agreement all around; more comments, questions, comparisons of past and present.

They talked for a long time, over breakfast, and I listened. There'll be more parties, I have few illusions. But I also am assured. We are all strong women, who watch over one another, together.

Hot biscuits and an open heart induce the finest conversations.

July 7: **Biscuit recipe**

2 cups flour
3 tsp. baking powder
1 tsp. salt
1/4 cup shortening
3/4 cup milk

Mix dry ingredients in bowl. Cut in shortening with a fork until it is crumbly. Stir in milk. Turn out on floured counter or board, pat with floured hands into a flat circle about an inch high. Cut into 8 wedges, place on ungreased baking sheet. Sprinkle with poppy seeds or sesame seeds. Bake 10 min. at 450°F. Serve immediately.

You can make these with whole-wheat flour, but they will lose the lightness that is their hallmark. Half whole-wheat and half all-purpose flour is a good compromise. Unbleached flour is fine, of course; and buttermilk if you have it makes these biscuits awesomely light. The recipe doubles beautifully. Just don't handle the dough too much.

July 8: **Fear**

Everyone is afraid. We bury our fear, we face it down, we find ways to live with it; but we are all afraid from that moment as a child when we realize our goldfish, our grandpa, or our parents can die.

This fear has its uses. It propels us into finding out what life is about. Later, as adolescents, we pretend life will go on forever and we almost fool ourselves. But underneath, there is a whisper. "What are you here to do? What is your song to be sung before you die?"

And so we learn our own peculiar song. We learn to live alone and in relationship. We learn to rejoice that we are alive, in this strange century, in this time that is, like all times before, cruel and lovely and not at all like the old days.

When our song comes clear, we see we have been singing through our fear all along.

July 9: **Leisure**

Sometimes, after a long period of work, it's impossible to contemplate leisure. It is as if my body has forgotten how to unbend from the desk and my mind has no idea how to occupy itself.

This is why humans need passions – someone we love, a garden that calls us, skiing, murder mysteries, cycling – something or someone powerful enough to call us away from habit.

If such a passion doesn't exist, it is necessary to invent one.

July 10: **Silence**

Most of us know that silence is necessary to heal our souls.

At camp we give up electricity and live with no sound but our own voices; the wind; the crackle of bacon on the morning fire (we plunge with glee into a high-fat diet, I can't think why), the splash as we hit the water, numb, for a pre-breakfast swim. Small sounds, compared to the clatter of civilization.

Oh, I'm not one to leave civilization. I love hot baths and movies, museums and airplanes...

But silence heals. We can hear the Spirit in it.

July 11: **Shadow**

I am always instantly (well, the next morning) alert when I have dreams of going to the movies. It's an old theater, usually, with an old-fashioned projector you can hear whirring away through the film / dream.

It's one of the less-subtle ways my dreams choose to inform me I am projecting material out of my own unconscious onto someone else. Oops, I say. Again.

Like everyone else on the planet, I have buried parts of myself that my parents or later my peers, my church, or my culture disapproved of. These parts live in my shadow, out of my conscious life. I don't know them.

But dreams tell me about them. So the morning after a "projector" dream, I ask myself: Who do I have unusually strong feelings about right now, who irritates me, puzzles me?

The name of a noisy woman comes up. How is that me? I wonder. Then I flip backward in time: there is a conversation in the schoolyard, long ago, and one of my friends is telling me I laugh too loud and talk too much. And I see suddenly how freedom of speech – my own noisy self – is tired of being held down in me, and wants out.

So the day after that dream, I say precisely what I think.

When we let our shadow live a little, we have more energy. And we are more whole.

July 12: **Incarnation**

We go looking for God. It's what humans do. Television evangelists find God easily. But since their glimpse of God's presence is often marked by an outrageous exclusivity – God seems to be white, male, heterosexual, well-to-do and Christian – I don't trust them.

But God does appear.

Last week, in my congregation, someone died. He had needed a food bank at one time, and had been a worker at ours. He was well-known in the community that gathers each Thursday for the food program. A local donut shop sends leftover donuts (I suspect them of making an extra-large batch Wednesday night) so it's a place to munch and visit.

It was decided to have his funeral on Thursday morning in the familiar gym and not the sanctuary, which would be strange to most. Because most of this group in our congregation has no money for suits, it was decided the officiants would not wear their formal robes. And some of this regular Thursday community made sandwiches from tuna and eggs that had been collected for the food bank.

I am sure that as the tuna and egg sandwiches were passed, and the bread was broken, God was there. Just as surely as at any communion service in any sanctuary. We find God in our neighbor, breaking bread.

July 13: **Writing**

Of all the creatures God created, we are the only ones who developed a great narrative to explain how we stole the knowledge of fire from the gods. We are the creatures who ate the apple and then – in language resonant with meaning – explained how we paid for that knowledge by being forever banished from the Kingdom of Innocence.

Writing words is a spiritual discipline given only to humans. Writing down a dream in the cold light of morning, imagining the words the dream-creatures would say. Confiding in a journal or a letter to a friend. Writing songs.

God lives where the words live, and when we write we join God there and ease the terrible loneliness of God. The Word becomes flesh and dwells among us.

July 14: **Irritation**

The people we love have a habit of exasperating us. When we know someone really well – because we are married to them, or linked by blood – all their faults are magnified in a most peculiar way.

And we aren't perfect in their eyes, either.

It's precisely because we love them, though, that we are irritated.We expect partners and parents to make us happy. Especially spouses. Burning in the flames of early romantic love, we projected superhuman qualities onto them. Married, we perceive reality. They are as weak and human as ourselves and they cannot create our happiness for us.

We might as well relax. We might as well accept their humanness, acknowledge their faults (to ourselves) and go on about the business of being friends as well as lovers. And happiness itself might slip in when we aren't looking.

July 15: **Dualism**

Somewhere along the way the notion of perfectability entered the universe, the idea that it's possible to be completely good, completely pure. It's an enormously damaging idea, especially for women who are looking for some spiritual truth.

Because the more we attempt to be completely good, the larger the parts we have stifled in order to be this way grow. Underneath, a small voice calls "let me out, I waaaaant..." and it grows more fierce the longer it is repressed.

It's the nature of humans to be good *and* bad, both wrapped up in one body.

We don't have to act on our dark impulses. We just have to be tender with ourselves, and them.

July 16: **Body**

Who of us could possibly love the body we live in? When perfectionism strikes, we berate it for being not perfect. When we are filled with anger-turned-inward, we feed our bodies to ward off the emptiness of depression. When we are filled with joy, we celebrate, and rightly so, with a feast. And then feel guilty.

We need to stop blaming ourselves. We've been taught not to love our bodies for thousands of years, from the purifying rituals found in scripture, to the Greek notion that the body is separate from, and lesser than, the mind.

But now we know better. We know mind and body interact, and that one is as valuable and spiritual as the other. God is not waiting to love us sometime later, when we are, as many believe we will become, pure spirit. God loves us in our miraculous flesh.

We need to enjoy this body. It's the only one we will ever have.

July 17: **Balance**

In winter, when I have been doing a lot of writing, or speaking – head work – I am compelled, zombie-like, into the paint store. I choose colors, check wallpaper, admire the patterns, visualize the way things might look.

In summer, I go out and dig wildly.

A life lived too much in the head, for too long, begs for compensation.

July 18: **Community**

Communities are circles of people. Sometimes, when we see the same people at work and at the

Home and School meeting, and the ski hill too, those circles overlap.

One of my favorites is a gathering of people that meets only once a year to put on a turkey supper, a massive fundraiser that involves more than 800 people by the time you include all those who are fed.

With my arms in greasy dishwater, I can see the meaning of life: people talking to one another, joking as they get tired, helping each other, caring for one another. The money we raise is important. But its most valuable aspect is the way it creates a community where it doesn't matter at all what you earn, how you dress, what your politics are. You just work and laugh together anyhow.

July 19: **Viriditas**

Annuals are more work for a gardener. You have to start them ahead of time, and fuss over the seedlings. But then, in summer, you put out all these little plants. And they sit there, innocent, until one day when you have your back turned they burst into raucous bloom and strangers stop to ask you what that silky blossom is (*Silver Cup Lavatera*) and whether those huge yellow daisies are sunflowers (*Indian Summer Rudbeckia*).

This is what the great mystic Hildegarde of Bingen called *viriditas,* greening power. She made up the word. It's the same as Dylan Thomas' "force that through the green fuse drives the flower," and the same as the Holy Spirit, the creative force that propels the universe.

In a rainstorm, I stand at an upstairs window and look out. I can see this Spirit moving through the Morning Glories creeping up the streetlight; the tall Blue Horizon Ageratum; the dusty grey foliage of the California Poppies with their silken glowing petals furled, but filled, like me, with *viriditas.*

Gardens gather people with their greening force.

July 20: **Lot's wife**

It's hard to be an apologist for God. God's behavior in the Bible is harsh enough to make you long for the old gods.

God is implacable with Sodom, raining sulphur upon it until it is reduced to smoking ash. And the wife of Lot, who heeded God's warning to flee but forgets the injunction not to look back, is most unfairly treated. She turns for one last glimpse of all she has lost in the slaughter, and is turned into a pillar of salt.

It happens. Lot's wife is part of us. That's why this story is so upsetting. Caught by the devastating, inherent unfairness of life, caught in divorce, loss, grief, pain, we look back and are paralyzed by our own salty tears. This story only tells us – in the way that nightmares do, as loudly as they can – the truth: go, go on, the world is lovely and cruel and there is no reasoning with it.

Lament is useful. Regret turns us into salt.

July 21: **Dreams**

A lovely thing happens when you find people you can trust with your dreams: you can begin to see your own unconscious.

Just as we can't see our own back without a mirror, it's hard to see our unconscious without others to reflect it back to us. They can do this by offering their own associations with the symbols in the dream. It gives us more to choose from, opens up symbols we may not see. And sometimes, just having a friend with us gives us courage to go farther into the dream.

Knowledge that is too much for us alone can be approached if we are accompanied by friends.

July 22: **What if?**

Two important words, what if. They unlock the mind and let us imagine new visions for the future by looking backward. Sometimes I imagine how it might have been if my people, the ones who started coming in boats from France and England and Scotland hundreds of years ago, had been good guests.

What if, instead of insisting their ways were best, they had obeyed the rules of the household which offered them hospitality? What if they had adopted the potlatch? Perhaps today we would live in a country where it is important to give away as much as you can. What if they had learned – like the Innu who honor the Caribou Masters when they kill one – to be grateful for the gifts of Mother Earth? Perhaps we wouldn't be wondering if pollution in our water systems is hurting our bodies. What if they had honored the shaking tent? Perhaps we would never make an important decision, one that would affect the community, without consulting our spiritual elders.

July 23: **Men and women**

It's only a framework. It's just that it works so well – Carl Jung's idea that every man has a feminine side, every woman a masculine side. Even as his idea of "contrasexuality" was offered and explained, the world was changing beneath his feet.

Now that theory has holes blasted through it. Our notions of what is "feminine" and what is "masculine" and how much biology determines those aspects have gone through convolutions that would have dizzied Jung's Victorian sensibilities.

Still, I cling to this architecture of the soul. It's a more solid framework than many and explains those moments when I suddenly know what men are trying to do and say, when I can feel it in some part of myself. It would be hard to understand one another at all without this little bit of otherness inside ourselves to show us how we are the same.

July 24: **Shadow**

Different things get put into the shadows of men and women. That's part of why gender-bending clothing is so interesting. It's an unconscious attempt to break down those differences.

For women, it is important to know what is in the male shadow as well as our own. Since the shadow is that part of themselves which men bury and hold down, it is often horribly distorted, and gets projected onto us in that way.

So male gentleness, male tears, all the tender emotions are buried in them as weaknesses. And when a woman gets up to speak – say, filled with tears at an emotional moment – men project weakness onto her, instead of the strength such tears can represent. For the same reason, some tough business leaders castigate "bleeding hearts" who make them feel the compassion they have locked out of their own hearts, and hence fear deeply.

Difficulties in relationships don't always start and end with us. Our position in a relationship with a man may be peripheral; he's really relating to his own shadow.

July 25: **Time**

It's a good idea to seek out the moments that have defined our lives. Sometimes they are hard to see because there may be pain attached to them.

Nations have defining moments. We all know that America changed when Kennedy was shot, Canada changed when a roadblock was thrown up at Oka. It's not so much reality itself that changed in those moments. That reality had always been there. But we were forced, as a people, to see it more clearly than before.

It is important to name the defining moments in our personal lives, when our grasp on what we thought was real loosens and slips away. Death or divorce takes someone deeply loved. A book or a conversation produces an idea deeply loved. The child produces a different value than our own, and our self-image as a mother takes a kick that changes our personal universe.

These moments cause us to rewrite our personal narratives. We can revisit those times later and see how they changed the rest of our story. Perhaps our narrative needs another draft. Personal myths are essential but not sacrosanct.

July 26: **Community**

Our middle son made the national triathlon team. That meant he suddenly needed $5000, for airfare to New Zealand and for the month-long training camp that preceded the event.

The first donation he received, after a short item about him appeared in the newspaper, came from the local chapter of the Independent Order of the Daughters of the Empire. It's a safe bet that most of its members had not, to this point, been deeply involved in triathlons. But he is a child of this city, of this community. The IODE contribution was slipped into our mailbox late that evening.

Other cheques and fundraisers followed. He went to New Zealand. A child of God, and the IODE.

Everyone needs extra grandmothers. A community is the best gift you can give your child.

July 27: **Seeking God**

I know God is after me when I wake up night after night with the same dream burning in my mind. I could ignore the call. But look where that got Jonah. (Into the belly of a whale, in case you haven't been around any Sunday school plays lately.)

So I swing my legs over the bed, reach blindly for my pen and any scrap of paper at hand, and write down the dream. (Far away, down in the lake, I hear a splash. The whale is swimming elsewhere.)

In the morning I read my midnight scrawl and ponder. Mostly God just wants me to notice something about myself, wants me to be a little braver or wiser or stronger.

It makes me a tad nervous, though. A wise and brave man named Bonhoeffer said that God always gives us the strength we need, but never too far in advance. What might God have in mind?

Selective deafness is not desirable with God.

July 28: **Hope**

Just a small item in the paper, but I could hear Eliot, "April is the cruelest month," sweeping through my body. Spring is cruel after winter, hope is cruel after long, freezing denial that we are in pain.

It was about a cure for the intractable illness that destroyed my brother's and my mother's sight. A long, long way away, and tenuous, but still a shred of hope.

Hope allows us to feel; and so I felt the grief I had pushed away, watching two people I love dearly journey into darkness. Watching their pain for each other, a lake of anguish we dammed up, or froze over, every day so we could go to work and school and cook the meals and do the laundry and laugh and argue and love life.

Unless we are very brave, we do this denial whenever we, or someone we love is hurt. But maturity can bring courage. We may learn to live in hopefulness again.

Every frozen feeling, if we are fortunate, will someday thaw and turn to tears.

July 29: **Conflict**

When we have a fight with someone, and want to get over it, a meeting alone for the first attempt is best. It is in a one-to-one meeting – without the need to save face in front of others – that a conflict has its best chance at resolution.

July 30: **Writing**

When I am in the middle of some large work, I

wake up at night seething with it. I write ideas, clear and pure at four o'clock.

This is why we write. For the excitement that curls through us in the dark, for the sudden clear hint of pattern in the story, when the words begin to spill like a river in the spring.

There is a moment, very rare, when you know this is what it is to be alive, every little brain cell jumping up and down and saying "yes."

That is why we write.

July 31: **Rage**

One of the most useful things I learned as a teacher was the power of surprise. Whatever you did that was out of the ordinary locked itself into the minds of students. For instance, getting mad. My teaching style is collegial, I hope gentle, I hope respectful of the human beings in front of me.

But about once a year, if my students were not working as well as I thought they might, I would allow some incident to evoke a good strong case of wrath (at everyone, never directed at one person).

My stomping around the room in righteous rage was such a shock it worked.

I think an all-out rant is a possibility once in a long, long while. If a relationship won't be damaged by it and if a group needs to hear something they aren't hearing. But only if it is desperately needed. Its entire power resides in it being out of character. A rant that occurs twice is boring.

AUGUST

August 1: **Trees**

I live in the shadow of a vast maple outside my window. This tree blesses me. In summer it cools the south side of the house, a canopy alive with chickadees and sparrows. In the fall, I exult in its blaze of red. It heads into winter with a passion I long to emulate, burning itself out in a rush of magnificence.

In return, I offer it no harm. No pesticides cloud the garden beneath. No paving starves its roots. And when its winter-bare branches scrape the glass on a windy night, waking me, I pray for its safety, as I would for any friend.

When I was a child, I talked to trees. Worried aunts told my mother I needed playmates. I had all the friends I needed, thanks, and now I talk to trees again. "Become as a little child," said Jesus. I'm working on it.

August 2: **Imagination**

If we cannot imagine a world in which the ozone layer is intact, how can we possibly work toward it? If we cannot imagine a world in which there are no food banks, how can we build it? If we cannot even conceive of a world where our daughters can walk at night without fear, how will we create it?

There are pictures of that world hidden in scripture.

It's why I go to church. Dimly, somewhere, in the collective memory of us all, there is a picture of a world in which the proud are scattered and the hungry are filled with good things. Sometimes it gets mentioned. And it unlocks my imagination.

August 3: **Wind**

God appears in dreams as wind. I grow rigid, days too filled with self-taught duty. At night my sleep is haunted by wind buffeting the windows, trying to break in.

I dream of tall apartment buildings, too high, like the Tower of Babel. Who am I to think I can reach heaven with hard work? Soon I'll be babbling in tongues.

The wind rocks the buildings. God is calling me.

I will go and lie in the grass for awhile, and watch the daisies moving with the wind. When the wind of God appears, it's best to find a place where it can blow through our hair.

August 4: **Seeking God**

The Celtic monks, St. Columba and St. Aidan and the others who crossed the sea to Europe in their little coracles, did so not because they wanted to leave home. They loved their little islands. They went because they were called to be pilgrims: to place themselves, body and soul, on the path to God.

In pale imitation of their impassioned wanderings, I climb into the bow of our battered green canoe each summer. Only the unrelenting tug of pilgrimage – and my husband, eager, in the stern – could pull me from my garden now, with the purple coneflowers, so frugal in their blooming, yearning for me to see them.

We are alert. The water whispers with our paddles and we listen with our hearts. Perhaps in a mist that rises from a silk-grey lake we'll see the face of God.

Sometimes we have to leave home to find our true home.

August 5: **God**

The clearest doctrine of God I've ever heard came from a then-seven-year-old named David Pace. He was with a small group of other church-going seven-year-olds and they had argued about who God was.

Finally came this child's wisdom, delivered slowly and carefully. "Nobody knows," he said. He was unworried, needing no more assurance that God was real (though unknown) than the churchgoing belief of his parents. "Nobody knows who God is. You can't know. Nobody knows what God is like. God's just God."

It requires raw courage or the simplicity of a child to note that the garments of orthodoxies and doctrines, creeds and statements in which we clothe our faith are only human-made. They garb inadequately a God seen dimly in our dreams or heard in contradictory inner voices many would discount.

All our doctrines may be wrong. The closest description we have of God may be the simple statement of a child.

August 6: **Balance**

One thing women have begun to gain is the right to work hard, to exhaust themselves, to neglect the house and forget to walk the dog and not always cook dinner, because they are absorbed in something creative.

It has been a long struggle, and it's not over yet.

A balanced life is very good. Now if someone could just explain that to the creative process...

August 7: **Women's genius**

Cleaning drawers, putting away clothes, I come across a dress my mother made for our then-infant daughter. My mother, until her eyes failed, was an inspired knitter. This dress is of cream-colored wool, intricately fashioned in the Aran Isle pattern for which she is famous.

Then I notice, as I fold it in tissue paper, a mistake. One tiny flaw, no one else would ever see it. But in the normal way of things, she would have. It should never have got past her. But it had. I hold the little dress up to the light, choked suddenly by tears. I had seen the moment that my mother, with her impeccable sense of style, her minute and loving attention to detail, her delight in her craft, began to grow old.

Genius is made of great skill and great love; it is the creative force of God emerging in humans, mothers, knitters.

August 8: **Grief and joy**

We are wrapped in grief, every day. If we are fortunate, we will note how – at this moment – we are filled with mourning. Our legs have grown harsh blue veins, our stomach is less flat, we have grown old. Or our child has been born, and we are now, forever, Mother. Or our children have left home. We don't want them back, no, not at all, but we miss them.

That mourning is only possible because we also know joy. If we are fortunate, we will note how – at this moment – a loved friend curls up in a chair to visit, a tree changes color outside our window, snow falls like lace on our coatsleeves, we have grown old and wise, our child is born, our child leaves home.

It's easy to see none of these things, neither grief nor joy. We chatter on about the weather while the greatest moments of our lives slip by unnoticed, unsifted, uncelebrated. The holy grail we seek is carried through our livingroom by a lovely maiden escorted by a hundred knights, while we are looking at the dust in a corner.

The wine of spiritual presence is poured into the chipped glass of everyday life.

August 9: **Hope**

When I was a child, I was given such a dose of hopefulness I have had to spend the rest of my life as an incurably hopeful person.

I don't mean optimistic. I mean that every situation carries hope inside it.

It comes from working with my father in his garden. I watched as – several times – he turned a small piece of Northern Ontario into paradise. I would work along with him, absorbing his stubborn belief that if you work long enough and hard enough, everything will be all right.

I know with my head that's not really true. But my heart remembers those gardens everywhere we moved, blooms springing out of wasteland under my father's hand. And I am filled with hope.

August 10: **Good and Evil**

Good and evil live inside us, both together. Mythologizers and novelists do their best to point this out. Anne Rice's vampires, for example, are heroes and saints, fallen and anguished and yearning to be good.

But we have long externalized evil.

I was in occupied East Germany shortly before the Wall came down. Out alone, I met some Russian soldiers marching along in loose formation.

I was terrified. There was no need. I was simply standing there, anonymous. They could have no reason to speak to me. It's likely their entire lack of German matched my own. In any case, although we didn't know it, the Cold War was nearly over.

But a thousand spy novels were lodged in my spinal cord, and I couldn't move. The North American notion of evil personified launched itself out of my body and projected itself onto these uniformed men. I might as well have seen the devil.

What we do not acknowledge in ourselves, we project outward. When a whole country does this, we create an evil empire.

August 11: **Contentment**

My boys went through a difficult stage when they were in their early teens. They told me what to write about. They wanted me to be a famous investigative reporter and win prizes for discovering – and disseminating persuasively – little-known facts that would bring down the government. They wanted me to be a best-selling novelist, preferably in the area or science fiction or murder. They wondered why I wasn't a famous broadcaster.

"I've been raising you and your sister," I said.

This was not enough.

"You are responsible for your own lives," I said. "And I am responsible for mine. You go ahead and be famous. I'll just do the best I can."

The balance between ambition (which, unfulfilled, can drive you mad) and contentment (which can leave you, well, financially impoverished) is fine and fragile and hard to see. We just do the best we can.

August 12: **Anger**

By nature, if I'm angry, I like to think about what caused it, and then create a clear and reasoned argument for not letting it happen again.

By the time I have gone through all that internal musing, the person I am angry with has forgotten what he or she did. Or I have become so enamored of my careful argument I've forgotten I've never said it out loud and I am quite surprised when the offending behavior happens all over again.

It is the way I was made. Sometimes I try to modify this. I admire people who can deal with a bad thing at once, crisply, especially because this is what popular wisdom says you should do. But when I try, it comes out badly.

Sometimes we have to deal with things our own way, not anyone else's.

August 13: **Healing**

One of the hazards for those who are chronically ill is becoming cut off from community. Few people want to deal with someone who is immersed in their own pain all the time, who can't see around it. It gets in the way of friendship.

Sometimes we become chronically ill in our souls, and that cuts us off, too.

In both cases, part of healing is the return to community. One of the most valuable aspects of dream work in a group – or any other kind of support group – is that it brings us back to human companionship and intimacy.

We can be healed, if not cured, by the presence of friends.

August 14: **Belief**

I have enormous difficulty with the type of preacher who exhorts me to believe in Jesus.

Belief is not an act of will. That's like saying, "Grow six inches taller and you will be beautiful." The reality is there, or it is not. Perhaps if the preacher said, "You look worried, can I help?" then I would believe. Not because he knew my worries, but because I could see the reality of that love he goes on about.

Evangelism, like good writing, is showing, not telling.

August 15: **Gaia**

It is morning and my husband is watching three moose splashing in the bog at the foot of Maple Mountain.

It is morning on a piece of the ancient web of earth and water and sky the Greeks called Gaia, and the people native to this area called Mother.

Like all Creation, Maple Mountain is both ordinary and holy. It is a cathedral rimmed with bog, and we have made our pilgrimage to it, crossing swelling open water and slipping through a shallow, winding creek to pitch our tent. My husband wakened early, hearing moose.

The circle we draw around what is holy grows large again. Once we forgot all this, we Christians. We believed that great stone churches were the only houses for which God yearned. But now we have remembered. We know that God loves all the earth and all Her creatures with holy abandon, holy passion.

August 16: **Angels**

American theologian Walter Wink tells how he was leading a youth group once. They were discussing the way Jesus suggested to the rich young ruler that he sell all he possessed, give it to the poor, and follow him.

The discussion was not going well. Finally, Wink looked around. They were in the kind of room you sometimes find in well-established churches in wealthy areas. There was a handsome oriental carpet on the floor that must have cost – he realized – over $10,000. And the rug was whispering, "Not true. Not true."

When an important conversation is going badly, look around. Something that can't speak may be contradicting you.

August 17: **Regret**

I cleaned my study and burned my first stories, weeping. I can't think why I did this, except that they reproached me by their presence, told me I wasn't good enough to get them into print.

Finally, I removed them. Regret, which is

all they had to teach me, is an emotion I do not need.

I suppose this is the way the Flood came into the mind of God. The rebuke of God's creatures, with their many imperfections, was too much for God to take.

God changed, after that. And so will I.

August 18: **Writing**

The movement of writing, for someone keeping a journal or writing a novel, article, or speech, is always the same. First you go down. Writers are consumed with the need to connect. That can't be done until you have gone far enough into yourself to find your own deep feelings. The connection takes place when the images you create and the pace of the narrative sets up a rhythm with the reader's own feelings, and there is recognition.

It's not that the reader has to agree, not even after reading the story. It's only that the reader must be persuaded to care.

August 19: **Denial**

Denial is my very favorite defense mechanism. People talk about it as if it were something of which to be ashamed. "You're in denial," is the phrase, said gently by someone who only wishes our good.

Yes indeed. Whatever gets me through.

I like dreams because they collude in this. They will be indecipherable until we are ready to hear their message. People who work on dreams together in groups should be careful not to baldly interpret someone's dream for them, lest they rupture that person's denial. It's not a great danger – mostly we will just refuse to accept any interpretation we aren't ready to acknowledge – but such behavior is wildly outside the delicate range of dream etiquette. Someday, when we are strong enough, we will acknowledge whatever reality is waiting.

Our soul knows how much truth we can handle, and offers us exactly that amount.

August 20: **Change**

My husband went to South Africa to help monitor their first elections. This filled me with confusion. I wasn't much worried about his safety; he had been in places of political unrest before and his habit was to return.

It's more that leaving home, allowing new experiences into our lives, always makes me fret. We change, each of us, when we are away. The person who came home after a month wouldn't be the same person who had left. Minute but necessary calibrations would occur in our relationship, and we would have to slowly, slowly, shift here and adjust there.

While he was gone, a package arrived – a generous bundle of flowers with a small figure tucked inside. A potter friend had sent me one of her clay angels. When I lifted it, the angel's copper wings shivered, a whisper of air that suddenly banished my unease. We are affected always by small things, the angel said. We are changed by the fluttering of a butterfly's wing at home or away. All the time. Every relationship. And we adjust.

August 21: **Scolding**

I've always tried not to scold. Then I went to England in 1989 to visit the women who camped at Greenham Common, the peaceniks who sat down in front of the big trucks that carried the Cruise missiles out for maneuvers.

They sat in front of the trucks and were dragged away to jail. They scolded their captors for warlike behavior. When they were released, they came back. They used heavy shears to cut through the fence at night and break into the guard-house to do their laundry. When the army tried to use geese to raise the alarm, the women fed them rum-soaked raisins until they collapsed in happy stupor, and broke in again. They walked arm in arm down the runway, declaring it was common land. They danced on top of the underground silos where the missiles were kept. They sang.

They scolded parliament, the military, an entire country that would allow such weapons to be launched. They stayed for six years, their numbers swelling on some weekends to over 30,000. They hung pestering signs on the fence. They were such a persistent irritant in the side of the men who ran

RAF Greenham Common (actually a US base) that they eventually won. The Cruise was removed.

I find it hard to be a nag. But sometimes you have to be one.

August 22: **Courage**

I used to think I was the only one who was afraid. As a journalist, I would hover over my words, afraid I hadn't used them in the best way I could, afraid I would hurt someone who didn't deserve it.

But after many years in the intimate atmosphere of dream groups, working with many different people, I realize I'm not the only one. Most of us are afraid. Most of us don't want to hurt people, don't want to be alone.

Courage and fear are not opposites, as I had always thought. They coexist, eying each other suspiciously. It's love that casts out fear, not courage. And we need to name proudly those times as women when we have been afraid and our courage has helped us tell the truth anyway.

August 23: **Letting go**

Perfectionist women find letting go especially hard because we like everything, well, perfect. But children don't grow up and husbands and lovers don't clean toilets until we get out of the way. (Don't laugh at that image. Toilets have been body work, dirty work, and therefore women's work; just as delivering babies and preparing bodies for burial has, through the centuries, been mostly women's work.)

Each of us has to decide whether relinquishing ownership so others in the family can pick it up is more important than a less-than-nutritious purchase when others do the grocery shopping or a few dust balls still rolling after the livingroom has been vacuumed. With a little practice, we find the extra time when we're not doing it all pleasant.

And learning how to relinquish what has long been our territory gives us a moral place to stand when we want men to give up the stranglehold some assume over the microphones in a large meeting, or the floor in a conversation.

August 24: **Unnamed losses**

Politicians talk about the Native "problem," the addiction and isolation and poor housing found on some reserves or in the inner city. I've never heard one talk about the richness we all have lost as a nation by allowing arrogance to steal away possibility. If the first people had been respected and the treaties honored, how much more earth-centered and whole we would be.

And women, there's a what-if there, too. How many skillful, creative people has business lost by being so inflexible that a parent gives up and leaves. How much wisdom does government lose when women are a tiny minority of those elected and placed in cabinet?

Sometimes we need to look at what didn't happen in our lives, and still could.

August 25: **Dreams**

Working on dreams in a group is very rich and intimate. We have all these hearts tuning themselves to our care, all these minds sifting images for us, offering associations and meanings for our perusal.

It's good to know how to set limits though, in a dream group as in any other highly intimate relationship. We humans love control so much, and so unconsciously. So the day will surely come when some well-meaning person will forthrightly say that "this is what your dream means."

They are wrong. "Thank you," you can say, "I'll consider that. But I need to choose the meaning of this for myself."

It's good practice for all the other times we need to choose for ourselves.

August 26: **Healing**

Storytelling is a form of healing. Every piece of children's fiction I have ever written floated up out of an encounter with a child's pain – my own remembered, or another's observed.

It doesn't mean the stories are sad. In fact, they are mostly happy. The jealousy provoked by the arrival of a small brother or sister is acknowledged and eased; the loss of a puppy or a goldfish is explored. Fear of being a wimp is resolved with an adventure.

Life is a risky adventure and we have no weapons but our own words. We name the wounds along the way and we weave them into a healing fabric.

August 27: **Prayer**

When we pray from our hearts we are on the right path. To pray, we must cut through bone and flesh to the part of ourselves that is most vulnerable, to the part grasped only dimly. We must talk to God from that part. It is the weakest, smallest, most fragile aspect of us that knows our truth.

All this is clearer for those who are poor. Their lives have been reduced to that essential. For those who are not, it is not so clear. They have to wipe away much to get to a place where they have anything to say to God.

August 28: **Water**

Water is a powerful symbol of emotional life. It is tears and the water of birth.

So when I dream of ice and snow I get nervous. Locked tears, frozen emotion, creativity and fertile thought trapped in chilly crystals. The dream is almost shouting: "Wake up, Snow White. Don't be rigid. Weep if you need to. Laugh, shout. *Lighten up.*"

Our bodies are 97 percent water. No wonder our souls like to swim in this image.

August 29: **Evil**

We resist evil by not joining it, by telling the truth, by praying, by naming it when we see it, by not going along with it.

One of the harshest things about the current economy is that some work too-long hours while others have no work at all. Those who work long hours find it hard to resist evil. They're too busy to see it. Those who are not working at all can see what it looks like – it's their child, hungry. But survival takes a lot of time.

Whoever said the devil loves idleness was wrong. Evil thrives when people are kept so busy they can't fight a cloud of meanness.

August 30: **Peace**

When Isaiah offered his vision of everyone living with their own vine and fig tree, everyone unafraid, he knew this was a true picture of peace. Peace is when all have land. Land held in common, like that of farmers in Chiapas, threatens no one, and there is no need for soldiers to burn the corn so people will move away.

The Cree in James Bay know this picture of peace, and the Innu in Labrador. They know they must not let the land be flooded, or reduced to something you fly over, something on which you practice bombing.

Gardeners bring the power of their imagination to this knowledge. From their grandmothers and grandfathers they have learned that peace and plenty are possible if you can only find some earth. So in their back yards, or on their balconies or windowsills, they fashion an alternate universe – different from the world – where the cycle of the seasons is revered, rightful decay is accepted, and labor is respected.

We women have long memories.We grow flowers because they remind us that peace and plenty are possible.

August 31: **Spiritual disciplines**

It's good to pray, walk, garden, write, dream. These are all ways to turn our face to God. They are all healing.

But God's face is also found in our neighbor. And our neighbor is not necessarily our friend, not necessarily the one who makes us laugh, not necessarily the treasured one who renews us, certainly not the person who lives next door. Our neighbor is simply the one who needs us.

That doesn't mean we have to give until we perish. That's what the praying or walking or gardening or writing or dreaming are for – to rest us. We take as much of those precious things, that precious time, as we need. Sometimes that's *all* our time; all we can do is re-create ourselves.

But then, one day, we will find our neighbor wounded by life. And we cannot pass by on the other side.

SEPTEMBER

September 1: **New life**

I had joined a Bible Study. I was a pretty serious student. We were working on the Gospel of Mark and a friend and I were given an assignment: to act out the story of the daughter of Jairus, the 12-year-old who dies while her frantic father is racing after Jesus, calling him to come and save her.

Jesus is delayed (a whole other story) and by the time he reaches the house of Jairus, the mourners are already wailing. But Jesus walks into the young girl's room and tells her to get up. And when, astonishingly, she does, he suggests she be given something to eat.

We acted it out. I was the daughter. And the most extraordinary thing happened. I suddenly remembered how it was to be 12 years old, to be intense and hungry all the time and filled with amazement at life. And I suddenly realized how long it had been since I had giggled.

It was as if this young girl had been sleeping or dying or dead in me, and when my friend said, "Little girl, I tell you to get up," she woke up.

I needed her badly. And she's never left me since. She's always sitting just below the surface of my life, saying, "Look. Oh, isn't that funny, isn't that amazing, isn't that wonderful?"

Isn't that funny, how a story will arrive just when it is needed?

September 2: **Bible**

I don't fully understand what scholars mean when they talk about historical criticism. I think they mean we need to look at the Bible critically, not literally, through eyes that understand the preoccupations of the day.

Or perhaps they mean we should look at our time, critically, from the vantage point of those who wrote the Bible. Those who wrote these scriptures might think us mad, with our determined individualism, our willingness to let some members of the community suffer while others have too much. Just as we think them bizarre to condone slaves and women covering their heads.

It's valuable to see our world through others' eyes.

September 3: **Identity**

We mothers need to have our own strong identity, because our children's suffering as they encounter life awakens our own pain. Especially around issues we haven't dealt with from our own past. It's hard to acknowledge their feelings, if we still can't deal with ours.

The first time I went to see my daughter play volleyball – she was in Grade Six – I saw this tall, awkward child out on the court, hoping the ball wouldn't come her way. I immediately started to cry. Suddenly I was back into my own clumsy childhood, where I was the big one who never seemed to make the grade on the gym floor.

I had never wept for that child. Even at my daughter's game, I choked back my tears, hoping she wouldn't see.

But after the game, I said, "It must have felt scary out there, with all those people looking at you."

The three of us – my daughter, the grown-up me, and the 11-year-old who still lives within me – had a long talk about how it feels to miss the ball sometimes. And we all felt better.

September 4: **Anger**

There's a persistent fire that gets into the muskeg not far from where I live, the vast peat bogs that cover much of northern Canada. It travels underground and smoulders for years, undeterred by rain or snow.

There are areas where smoke hangs in the air when it's quiet, biting at your throat.

Some kinds of anger are like that. Women are still more likely than men to internalize their anger, to let it smoulder underground like the muskeg fires, not quite going out for lack of oxygen, not quite burning itself out in a good strong blaze.

You'd think we'd be beyond it by now, but we're not. Too many centuries of hiding our anger, too much to lose if we let it blaze.

So when you dream of smoke – a smoky stove, a fireplace that draws poorly – glance around and see what you've done with your anger. If it has gone inward and downward, like the muskeg fires, you may want to do some digging. If it's so far down you can't see it, a therapist can help you excavate.

Half-remembered anger makes it hard to breathe.

September 5: **Angels**

I am touched by people who have been saved by angels, shoved back on the stairway when they have slipped, pushed closer to the dock when they are in danger of drowning. Angels appear as animals, or as shining figures, or are heard as music, or materialize – in the case of a friend of mine – as a little old lady in a grey coat.

I believe these stories profoundly. Sometimes I know the storyteller well and know a lie would be completely out of character. Other times I am simply convinced by the transparency of both tale and teller.

But sometimes I witness ordinary people, as knocked about by life as anyone else, being immeasurably kind to one another. That too, is a miracle. Angels appear in odd places.

September 6: **Spirituality and everyday**

One mark of Celtic Christianity – which flourished in Ireland and Scotland and the monasteries of England and Europe from about the seventh to the ninth century – was that the spiritual was not separated off from the rest of life. It was all of a piece. Everything was permeated with faith.

Perhaps that time is returning. The notion that spirituality is something for Sunday, that somehow God doesn't live in the everyday world, is coming apart. Churches that have tried to contain God and make God play by certain rules, defined by a few, are breaking into little pieces too.

And God is bursting forth, delighted to be free.

September 7: **Work**

Sometimes when work takes over everything else in our lives (or what used to be our life, when we had one) we do have to look at what's going on. Achievement can be just one more mask, just another way of defining ourselves when we are afraid to let the world see who we really are.

Women are more than our roles as mothers, as wives, as daughters. And we are more than our work.

September 8: **Gratitude**

In Northern Ontario where I grew up, it was and is the custom still, for some, to augment the meat in the freezer with moose or deer.

We receive the occasional gift of venison. My daughter annually marks her return from a stay at a friend's camp by triumphantly frying up a massive platter of fresh pickerel, her own catch.

Our family is urban now, university-educated, professional. Everything our grandparents dreamed we might be when they made that long boat trip from the British Isles most of a century ago. But I hope we learned something in those years when the making of a blueberry pie began with an old wire-handled honey can.

Gratitude.

We are grateful to the poplar for the paper in our books, the rivers for the hydro that runs our computers, the animals who feed us and share their habitat with us. Those who are grateful for what the earth offers take only what she can safely give.

September 9: **Finding God**

God is elusive, like a deer. The way to find God is to place ourselves on the path God uses a lot, and hope God will pass that way. And to be quiet, of course. You can only hear the leap of a deer or the breathing of the universe in silence.

September 10: **Love**

It's hard to love unless we have been well-loved enough to consider ourselves lovable. That's what is meant by "good-enough" mothers. Mothers don't have to be perfect. They just have to be good enough to let us know we are lovable.

If we haven't attained that much self-acceptance, it's important to find it. The best place to look is around people who love easily.

Volunteer organizations are logical places for people who are overflowing with love. Or children, who don't guard their love and are too young to have decided love must be perfect.

Some churches, if they understand that grace is more important than rules, can be filled with very loving people. You'll be able to tell by the way people treat each other whether or not this is case.

The way to learn to love is to go where we will be loved.

September 11: **Myth**

Those of us who have no myth must find one for ourselves. If we don't, the vacuum within will be filled by a story about the world that has no heroes, no journey, no grail. It will be all wilderness and no manna, no mountain.

It's not so hard to find a myth. That's what ancestors are for. If you don't know who they are and what the long story of your family might be, ask your grandmother or your great-grandmother to come to you in a dream. They can tell you where to find your story.

September 12: **Hospitality**

A good welcome isn't made by having a spotless house or even wonderful food, although those things are pleasant.

Mostly, hospitality is – as theologian Henri Nouwen says – a matter of clearing a space in our hearts for the person who is entering. That means looking at their face to see what expression is there. And listening – not just to their words – but the weight and tone and pace of them. It is being quiet. When people are in need and don't know it, a little silence will let the need surface.

We can let the need or pain or worry swim around for awhile between us, letting itself be seen and heard. And then we can let some of our own pain join it, to give it company.

Later we can take these worries on a long walk. Often the pain and worry become too tired to accompany us home and we can leave them on a bench somewhere to rest.

September 13: **Holy stories**

Spirituality suffers when we demand too many of what we are pleased to call facts. The strength of religion depends on its ability to deepen our lives, making them larger and richer and more complicated. That is intuitive work. It depends on living symbols that shift and turn according to our lives in that moment.

When religion becomes filled with rigid categories and rules, people rightly turn to what is open. The *I Ching*, the Tarot, the Medicine Wheel: all are alive because we have not stifled them with rules.

We can, however, take comfort. The stories of Sarai and Abram, Jesus and Mary, the birth and the healings, are far too large to pin down. Nothing can stop us from entering into the stories and receiving them into us, until their wisdom can sustain us.

September 14: **Male energy**

Often, when I have to drive a long distance, I play tapes by male singers Bruce Cockburn, Lennie Gallant, John Prine. Maybe I just want to hear gritty lyrics. But a friend of mine says she needs their aggression to get through traffic, and I think she's right. I sing along loud, and they help me think male. A certain attitude, if you have a long drive and transport trucks coming at you, can get you through.

September 15: **Authority**

It's sometimes hard for women to make themselves heard. The habit of not raising our voices runs deep. And the cheerful tendency of some men to assume they have something to say, and use up all the time available saying it, edges us out of public forums.

But we have remarkable talent to draw on. We know how to hear what those who can't talk yet are saying, a gift of intuition public life could use. We know how to do several things at once: soothe the baby on our shoulder, stir the soup, check on the toddler, pass the four-year-old another batch of playdough, listen to the friend in need.

Since we've seldom had a great deal of power, it's possible for us to have something better. Compassion.

And because we've mostly upped briefcases and gone back to work, we know how to balance careers with all that. We have, therefore, authority. But we'll need to assume it for ourselves.

September 16: **Sons and brothers**

Consider fathers, sons, and brothers. They are the people we might have been had we been born male instead of female. What they are like, how they handle stress, aggression, anger, relationships, frogs, toads and pieces of machinery offer us a glimpse of our own inner male principle.

September 17: **Faith stories**

It would be hard now to live away from the lake. Its place in my consciousness would leave a gaping hole if it were ripped away. When I need clarity I go there and look out. There is wind and space.

And time. Sometimes it becomes another lake with less-treed, drier shores, and a figure that walks over it. Sometimes the fishing boats have come forward from another century and the ring of stones that is a firepit just off the trail on a western beach could be one where a man who was supposed to be dead stood on shore and called to his friends: "Come here, have breakfast."

I bring these stories home from another century and make them mine. They give shape to my life. I don't know how this is. But I know it would be hard to leave this lake.

September 18: **Perennials**

I divide perennials in the fall. Spring finds them full and rounded and quite independent, and I can spend my time cunningly inserting annuals between them.

I set to work with my knife, dividing clumps of hosta and Shasta daisies. (All the sharp knives in the kitchen migrate out to the garden in fall. They make their way back in as soon as the ground is frozen; I don't cook much in dividing time, anyhow.)

No matter how innocent the clump, it produces hundreds and hundreds of offspring, all looking for a home. There is no need, I think as

I try to give them away to the neighbors, for such extravagance.

Clearly, God's plan is to have more than enough, to make sure the world continues.

September 19: **Success**

Many women are highly successful and don't know it. Success isn't tied to money. The most worthwhile activities are either unpaid or underpaid: caring for children, looking after elderly relatives, agitating on behalf of a river or the poor.

A successful life is full of unpaid but valuable work, balanced with enough paid work to keep us fed and clothed and sheltered. A successful life has time for walking with a friend while she pours out her soul, time for fragile and useless things like flowers.

A successful woman has found a community where she can be loved; not necessarily a husband, or children, although that might be so, and not necessarily an upscale suburb. Just a circle of friends where she is loved and her work admired.

It's important we define success in our own terms.

September 20: **Righteousness**

Mostly, I think of myself as a social justice type. I believe in protecting the vulnerable, especially the children, instead of the rich.

But every once in awhile, I meet someone for whom that is not enough. Their judgment, implicit or overt, hits me like a slap in the face.

This teaches me something. That arrogance and self-righteousness are nearly always vices; that tolerance and patience are usually virtues; that those who simply love, and do not speak of justice at all, often practice justice more fully than those of us who – by nature or by profession – rant.

September 21: **Writing**

Writers work alone but are utterly dependent on their community, not only to be their readers, but to be the actors in the constant drama writers observe. That's why writers are often cranky. If they are with you, they want to be at home writing what they thought they heard you say. But if they are alone, they fear slipping through the crack between their memory and the printed page.They never stop observing themselves and others, which makes them tired. Only compassion can save them.

September 22: **Knowing**

Women know reality the same way men do, of course. Because someone teaches us certain things in school, because we have observed certain things in our family and our peers.

And we also know reality through our bodies, as men do. But that means we know it very differently. Most of us don't play football. Most of us *do* give birth, nourish children through our bodies, and care for them with a combination of intuition and hope. Those of us who don't do this are still affected by it; it is the reality of our mothers. This is what we observed as we were making up our minds about how to be a woman.

It's hard to make such matters, children and the care of same, public realities, public concerns. They are so domestic, basic, private, seemingly intangible in a world of deficits and interest rates.

But women know they are all that is real.

September 23: **Work**

If we imagine that being hard-working or conscientious or loyal will make us successful financially (which is the way success is usually defined by the world) we are not wise. It won't. There are no guarantees for such success at all, except possibly being born rich.

So – once we're past the basic needs for food and shelter that we need our work to provide – it's no use doing it for the financial rewards. It's better to be driven by a passion for the work itself. Then, if success ignores us, we will have much pleasure (if not money) all our days.

September 24: **Seeking God**

Some women seek God in church. Others have found organized religion to be a straitjacket, restraining their connecting with God because the image of God it offers is so alien to who we are. Sometimes the weight of expectations and orthodoxies is too heavy, and we have to leave church for awhile, or permanently.

"Church" is always specific, too. Unless we live in a city large enough to have many churches, we are at the mercy of the way it appears in its local expression. If a local congregation is paternalistic or judgmental, and its images exclude women, it will be hard for us to make it our spiritual home – even though we know there are congregations elsewhere that regard women with respect and tenderness.

There's hope, though. Perhaps it comes from the constant internal balancing that goes on in humans. When our souls are not fed we get restless and seek nourishment elsewhere. We talk. We try crystals, therapeutic touch, dreams. We read about angels.

Some will laugh at this. Some will say it is dangerous.

Of course it is. Any quest, including that for faith, is always a heroic venture. There will be false voices to enchant us on the way. But every hero eventually finds true friends who accompany her and who help discern the truth.

September 25: **Dreams**

I never met a dream, from anyone, that didn't have something to teach me. When women work on dreams together, there is a particular ease in slipping into the others' dreams. Women share so many issues, as men do with each other too.

But it's also very easy to project ourselves into another woman's dream and take it over, seeing our own issues in it, making it ours, offering an interpretation that would fit for us, but not for her.

That's why men can be helpful in a dream group. They know they are in foreign territory with a woman's dream. They are careful. And sometimes – out of what Jung calls their anima, their own feminine side – they will ask the innocent question, the naive question, that helps it all make sense.

September 26: **Names**

In some Native communities, a child is not given his or her true name until the elders have watched for awhile to discern the child's nature.

There is wisdom in this.

The name we are given is important. The work new parents undertake, poring over lists of names and looking in books, is serious. Giving a child the name of a grandparent is significant.

A name is filled with a spirit who must be reckoned with as the child grows.

September 27: **Holy Spirit**

When we are feeling cynical about politicians in particular and institutions in general – and there is an infection of cynicism abroad – it's comforting to remember that we are not led by the Tories or the Grits, the Reformers or the New Democrats. We are led by God. And God will certainly tell us what to do, and send us earnest passion with which to do it.

September 28: **Jesus**

I like the baby Jesus very much. The infant asks little of me, only that I listen to the song of the angels and have a hand-out ready for a hungry shepherd.

This grown-up man is a different story. He commands me to love my enemies.

When I tell him this commandment makes life too hard, he takes me down to the lake. There is sand and beachgrass, and I can see a loon out where it's deep, hustling her babies through the waves. He holds out his hand. "Life is not hard at all," he says. "Come on." I hold his hand and we walk to the loon, waiting in earnest wonder.

Nothing is impossible with God.

September 29: **Autumn**

It's fall, and we are tidying the garden for the winter. I have saved a few geraniums to blossom on my winter windowsill, standing in for spring, for life, for the coming reign of God.

My husband moves vast barrowsful of leaves, marches to the compost pile with the day's vegetable peelings. We are assured the Shalom – the time when the earth will be healed and whole – depends on the energetic munching of lifeforms we can hardly see.

The pile grows large. Soon the snow will come, the earth will sleep.

And I say a prayer of thanksgiving for our growing closer to God. Yes, and closer to the earth.

September 30: **Cities**

Like many who grew up in small towns, I harbor a distrust of any place too big to get around by foot or bicycle. But I love the clever buildings of the city – especially the homes, both the beautiful and the wildly idiosyncratic. And I love the way green breaks out in the city, planned, or in waste spaces that spring up energetic weeds when no one is looking. The first time I ever went to Toronto, I looked out from what was then a vantage point, the Park Plaza Hotel, and wondered at the urban forest.

I love the complexity, a thousand different vital communities overlapping and interacting. I love the neighborhoods.

Some theologians say the city is holy, these crowded streets as sacred as a quiet lake. The city is as much a creation of God's loved creatures as anthills and beehives – and therefore just as much beloved.

OCTOBER

October 1: **Adulthood**

My mother has courage. She complains about her arthritic bones and her unreliable stomach, but never about her faltering vision. She wears that with the same stubbornness that insists on knowing what is on the labels, the same pride that would cheerfully rip the entire back out of a newly knit sweater. We can meet as adults, if I am not too distant, protecting myself, denying. And if I can get over my guilt that I don't visit her every day, the way she visited her mother, maybe I can learn that courage too.

Mothers and daughters are knit together by guilt and love. The first, with enormous difficulty, can be erased; the second, never.

October 2: **Inner dialogue**

Talking to yourself gets bad press, but it's a good idea. Any dream figure, indeed, any character who keeps entering your mind, while you are asleep or awake, can be part of a fruitful conversation.

It sounds trite: "The people we meet become part of us." But like many sayings that have become part of the lexicon of daily speech, it has a truth everyday use obscures. We think about people, dream about people, because something about them has meaning for us, stands for something active in us. They become a way for us to name aspects of ourselves we otherwise couldn't see.

I used to dream of Nazis. The drive for absolute perfection they embodied so tragically, the evil that consumed them, was putting me at risk as well. I couldn't see it, until my dreams chose this urgent way to convey the message.

Now I try to be more gentle with myself. My garden is allowed weeds; my children, my spouse and myself our failures. "You're not in charge here," I say to the Nazis within. "Begone."

But I am alert. They could come back.

October 3: **Framed**

Many of us go to work and stare at a computer screen. We drive home, peering through a windshield. In the evening, we watch a television screen. Sometimes we check the weather on it, instead of standing outside and looking at the sky.

Our days are framed and lit for us. All is seen through glass, edged, circumscribed, defined.

It's a good idea to plant a garden, as wild and uncontained as possible.

October 4: **Faith**

Each of us creates our own faith for ourselves. Christianity, for example. Really, there are as many Christianities as there are Christians. They all have Jesus in common. But his own question, "Who do you say that I am?" has a multitude of answers, not all compatible with one another: brother, friend, savior, God, redeemer, servant, sacrifice, revolutionary, King.

We each have our own answer to that question, and our own understanding of what the answer means. And then we add other bits to our faith, constructing a framework of belief from hymns and country songs, Bible verses, stories we heard in Sunday school and things our grandparents told us.

If we are lucky, our faith is created, too, from long afternoons spent in a hammock gazing at trees, and in arguments with people we admire. Some are fortunate enough to have visions that add to the structure of faith. And how we are treated by Christians when we are vulnerable helps create our faith, one way or the other.

We can never assume, when we talk about God, that everyone has the same God in mind. This makes life interesting, and sometimes hard.

October 5: **Obedience**

Women – especially mothers – need to cultivate steady self-esteem. Having a strong sense of self means we are able to cope with children who stand up to us without getting too upset. Mothers want kids who can stand up to adults. We want them to be able to say no to anyone in any position of authority who wants to take advantage of their lack of power.

Part of our mothering, as our children are very young, is getting them ready for the time when they will be swimming, or adrift, in a culture that is dangerous for them.

Not obedience, but clear-headed, thoughtful cooperation is needed. Resistance, questioning, and a clear sense of boundaries is very good for us, and our children.

Obedience is a vastly overrated virtue in women and children.

October 6: **Cleaning**

October is the quiet month of garden cleaning. The last annuals are pulled and taken to the compost heap. Clay pots are put away. A now-leafless bush reveals, under a branch, the pruning shears that were lost in June.

Perennials – especially the ones that were divided in September and hence look mangy – have their foliage neatly trimmed. The leaves are raked, except on the flower beds at the front, where they are left to protect the plants from street salt.

All is orderly and peaceful. Waiting. October is a fine time. All is reduced to strong shapes. Winter will soften the sharp outlines, but now we see the essence of the garden.

Our souls require this clean quiet after the noisy color of the last half-year.

Much of any joy – not just the garden variety – exists in the memory of it.

October 7: **What if?**

It's good that women are encouraged to have faith in their own thinking. We spent too many years listening to others, and we are right to trust our own wisdom at last.

But having too firm a grip on what we think

is right can make it hard to toss it away. And there is no true wisdom without turning our worldview upside down and shaking it. It's like those little snowscenes under glass, you turn them over and a storm begins. After awhile things settle, of course, but you have seen there are other ways the world might be.

October 8: **Change**

We cannot make the people we love different from what they are. We cannot change them. We cannot make perfect children nor a perfect spouse.

God can transform, of course, if God desires, and in God's own good time. But God's notions of perfection and our own are notoriously at odds. God, in fact (being their Creator), may feel any children or spouse with which you are blessed are fine.

We could work on changing ourselves, if we like. But God may like us, too, just the way we are.

October 9: **Finding wood**

Today we split the pine that fell across the path
Chopped up the birch that looked dead
(It wasn't quite.)

We walk along the road collecting wood
that falls off lumbertrucks
Our love sustained by fire
not roses.

October 10: **Eve and apples**

I love the produce store. Neat pyramids of potatoes and peppers, tomatoes and cucumbers, squash and broccoli, oranges and bananas. And apples, fresh and crisp all year thanks to the miracle of modern storage.

I always buy apples. I fill my bag with McIntoshes, sometimes Northern Spies if I'm making pie. And I think of Eve, punished for apples.

I gather them, polished, shiny, into my bag, there in the produce store, and I celebrate Eve's courage and I salute her choices: knowledge over ignorance, risk over submission. Real life, with all its complicated choice and pain, over sheltered innocence forever.

And then I go and buy potatoes.

October 11: **French apple pie**

Make pastry for one-crust pie and line 9" pie pan. Mix 3/4 cup sugar, 1 heaping tsp cinnamon or nutmeg, and 6 to 7 cups sliced pared apples. Heap into pie shell. Dot with 1 1/2 tbsp butter. Sprinkle with a crumbly mixture of 1/2 cup butter, 1/2 cup brown sugar (packed), and 1 cup flour. Bake at 400°F for 45 to 55 min.

October 12: **Sadness**

We shouldn't try to recover from our blue days before they have had a chance to teach us what they want us to know. They may be trying to tell us we are missing a friend who needs a call. There may be a little tug of rage inside that needs to be acknowledged. Or maybe there is something we need to do:

write a poem, pitch a tent, ride a horse, pick a flower.

Prozac and its cousins are a gift. But we shouldn't let ourselves be bribed into premature contentment.

October 13: **Pride**

If you were to go to some churches, you would note a general confession of sin at the beginning of the service. This is a piece of wisdom. God can certainly cope with our troubled feelings, and we feel better if we tell someone.

The sin of pride is, in some churches, a large item in this confession. Many women have trouble with this, and they have a point. Lack of confidence is more of a problem for women than arrogance, and self-effacement more our habit than inflation.

But one item. Just in case. Much of humanity has thought for many years that they are in charge of all the other creatures. That is overwhelming pride. We are only *one* of the animals: clever with our hands and nimble of brain, but prone to backaches and neuroses.

Perhaps women already know this. But if we don't, if we think we are above Creation, and not in it, our eventual death will come as a terrible surprise.

October 14: **Writing**

The best writing comes out of darkness; we've all known that since Satan got to be the chief player in *Paradise Lost.* The compressed energy of the deepest realm of the unconscious barrels like a freight train from a tunnel when it is released into words.

And writing things down heals the soul. It honors what has been hidden, dying, and gives it a voice and brings it back to life.

Journal writing is very fine for that, especially at first. But ultimately writing craves an audience. Humans desire to speak with one another; it's an urge as old as drawings on cave walls. We are knit together by our need for human response.

October 15: **Writing**

Writers don't tell; it's a rule as old as the craft. They show. Even the most non-fictive essay requires the evidence to bubble up as if unbidden. Writing is created out of images and snatched bits of conversation skillfully chosen to convey what the writer wishes, without telling.

Always our thoughts come in as an offering, not as hectoring. The latter is read only with masochistic pleasure by those who were yelled at whenever they sat down to read, and now understand it to be a humorless activity.

October 16: **Envy**

The hardest emotion to deal with is the clawing and largely unacknowledged feeling when someone seems to receive what we want and don't have.

But we are human, and envy, in its complexity and power, is the most human of emotions. Forgiveness of self is what's needed. It may help to remember that each of us has our own dance, our own life. We can't live anyone else's, no matter how lovely it looks.

October 17: **Religion**

Sometimes we think we can't wear more than one label at a time. But we can. I am Celt, Christian, and born-again pagan all at once. It comes from gardening, I guess. Every plant and every tree has its own spirit in it, and those spirits scorn the notion they must worship only one peoples' God.

October 18: **Messages**

When my computer crashed unexpectedly the other day – I was almost finished a huge, long article and I was late – a friend commiserated. "And what does it say to you," he said, "that it crashed." He's always trying to get me to drink less coffee and rest more, too.

"Nothing," I growled.

But he is right, of course. Sometimes the universe, or God, sends us a message. If we won't hear, God breaks the washing machine, crashes the computer.

Just a little longer God. I promise.

October 19: **Compensation**

A friend who works for the military pointed out years ago, shaking his head, that for a nice woman I sure go to a lot of violent movies. (We were discussing Oliver Stone's *Full Metal Jacket* at the time.)

We niceniks need depth to balance out our charm. When much of our lives are lived civilly, something inside us wants me to know it still lives.

And like our nursery rhymes that originated in the time of the Black Death, *"hush-a, hush-a, we all fall down,"* this is a way of defeating the terrors that surround us, by reducing them to manageable celluloid form.

October 20: **Personality type**

In our bedroom there is a large, damp patch on the ceiling. It's beginning to dry out now, and soon we'll get it painted. But the roof leaked, in that one place, for several months.

This is because this house is run, owned and looked after by two intuitive types. Intuitive-feeling types, to be exact.

Differences in personality between wife and husband are sometimes trying; similarities can be downright dangerous. The ceiling might have fallen in on our heads. As intuitives, we are both blessed with an outrageous ability to live "as if." It leads to a triumph of optimism over reality: we looked at the spreading patch on the ceiling and imagined it gone.

And indeed, when it wasn't raining, it was gone. The bubbling paint was a small detail that would – we said to each other – probably not get any worse.

Then we went off in pursuit of the meaning of life, which is how intuitives prefer to spend their time. It took the heavy rains of autumn to drive home the error of our ways.

The roofer came and went. And we'll get the ceiling painted, soon...

Where we are similar, we women and our friends, it is pleasant. But sometimes our differences are needed to complete each other.

October 21: **Getting along**

Getting along in a marriage doesn't happen because of love. Love is a help in that early period when the other is perfect and everything he wants is quite fine, quite fine.

But later, love doesn't help you get along at all. People who love each other very much can argue their way to divorce.

What makes a marriage or any relationship work is respect. Love gives it excitement and joy and is entirely necessary. But respect makes it work.

October 22: **Aging**

My friend dreamed of climbing a hill and discovering an attractive woman, about 60 years old, sweeping sand. The woman was wearing a medieval dress and living by herself in a small trailer parked nearby.

We talked about the dream in our small group. People gently asked questions, offered associations (was she a witch? was she a gypsy?) wondered if alone-ness and solitude had anything to do with it.

Finally we began to look at the trailer. How big was it, someone wondered. "Oh about 40 by 10," she answered with the matter-of-fact certainty that sometimes comes with a dream.

"And if you add it together, what does that make?"

"Fifty," she said.

And how old are you? was the next question.

"Fifty," she said.

There was a great burst of laughing recognition, of delight at the power of discovery in dreams.

"And what would it be like, living in the 'middle age'?" came from someone who had heard that word "medieval" with particular attention.

Again, a shout of delight from the whole group. Dreams are full of puns and number play...

October 23: **Aging**

... At last, with the group waiting in hushed anticipation, my friend shut her eyes and went inside the trailer, telling us what she saw like an undersea explorer sending messages back to the surface.

First she saw nothing. Then, gradually, she began to make out thick cushions and fine rugs, rich and glowing burgundies and greens, then a crystal chandelier – all in great contrast to the desert she had been sweeping patiently and not unhappily outside.

We talked for a long time about my friend's dream, about Jung's notion that middle age is the time when people are drawn to discover the richness of the inner life. About the lack of a toilet or sink or stove in this trailer that is symbolic of her life. There is no need; the inner life it describes is of the spirit, not the body.

It was a rich dream of affirmation for a woman whose whole life has been outward-oriented, but whose half-century mark invited her on a new journey to the depths of her own, beautiful, middle-aged self, where the healing qualities of not one crystal, but an entire chandelier awaited her.

This happens to many of us at menopause.

We begin to balance a life filled with business and housework and care for others, with our own spiritual development.

It's time.

October 24: **Sin**

Women don't inherit sin. Not from Eve and her apple, anyway. But a little closer to home, perhaps, and shared with men.

My ancestors in the faith were so sure they were right, when they came to this country. For 100 years, they ran schools for Native children. The children lived there, so they could be better made to be like other Canadians. The schools were funded by government, but not nearly adequately, and – especially in the early years – they were terribly crowded and tuberculosis moved through them like an angel of death. The children were hungry and badly dressed and beaten for speaking their own language and sometimes sexually abused.

This is as close as I can come, so far, to original sin. I cannot walk away from being Canadian or Christian. I inherit this country with the wildest beauty on earth, inherit this faith that keeps me whole. So I also, collectively with other citizens, inherit this sin.

October 25: **Wilderness**

Sometimes we have to walk into the not-knowing, into ambiguity. We have to live with neither seeing the truth in a situation, nor understanding what is the right thing to do. We might not have to live in this uneasy state forever. But moving out of it takes time. We need to use all our human ability to discern, to seek advice, to weigh conflicting demands, to reckon with – but not follow blindly – authority.

We have the gospel to help us. Like any great narrative, though, it can yield conflicting truths. So we have to suffer the terror of not being sure of what to do while we wait for it – and prayer and our friends and our own experience – to speak to us.

This terror can't be lifted too quickly. We have to sit in it for awhile, and that's harder for some of us than for others. It helps if there *are* others, and we can wait for clarity together.

October 26: **Communion**

Always there are these words. "This is my body, broken for you. This is my blood, poured out for you." Bread is passed, and then wine.

I have no idea what is happening here, no idea at all. It is a mystery and I am filled with awe. People I know well, who are my friends, pass little trays filled with bread, tiny cups filled with wine. They are solemn, careful, like children trusted with a birthday cake.

In the choir we sing:

"Eat this bread and never hunger,
drink this cup and never thirst,
Christ invites us to the table
where the last become the first."

All this attention to a tiny piece of bread. A tiny piece of the broken world and – at the same time – a symbol of the world healed by the love of God.

Who could know what this means? Who

could ever understand love? I have no idea. I only know these people here, my friends and I, are – just for a moment, on a chilly Sunday morning in autumn – whole.

October 27: **Work**

We have a right, as women, to immerse ourselves in our work sometimes. Recently I emerged from a difficult series of deadlines to discover I had been absent in my own house. The fridge looked the way it looks when I have been away for awhile. Unloved. And no one had thrown away dead flowers; they sat in vases all over the house.

But these are *my* obsessions, after all: cushions plumped in a certain way, flowers everywhere, food. The people with whom I live have their own obsessions, so I wasn't blaming them. Just bemused by the way work can absorb me.

Women's lives are more complicated and rich and interesting than even the most fascinating career. Still, at last we know it is our right –

as much as it is the right of men – to give ourselves to work we love.

October 28: **Rituals**

Sometimes an insight from a dream will ask for a ritual. When a dream pointed out to me an imbalance in my life between home and away, family and career, I went out to buy wallpaper for the kitchen.

Such a simple ritual, hanging wallpaper. No chanting (except what comes when the inevitable difficult patching takes place, this kitchen's walls are singularly uneven); no burning (except what comes with the first charred toast). Just going to the store and ordering this paper, dark green like a garden and covered with apples.

I will be Eve in this kitchen, peeling and carving the fruit of the Tree into pies and sauce and apple crisp, giving away the secrets of life.

Small domestic rituals have the power to balance a lop-sided life.

October 29: **Courage**

Once I dreamed a voice from heaven said, "I'm going to finish you now," and a steel rod was pounded down my back.

It was not a pleasing dream. But I think it was a good one.

All my life I have prayed for courage, like the cowardly lion. But there was never any wizard, until that voice. I think that was the day (or rather night) God decided that – like a fine piece of furniture or a debutante at finishing school – I might as well be completed. I was given a backbone of solid steel.

I don't bend as much in every breeze as I used to; I'm getting older and a little clearer about who I am. And when I'm scared, I remind God about that dream.

October 30: **Identity**

We don't fully choose our identity. Some of it we can change, most of it we can't. I was born in Northern Ontario and raised as a Protestant Christian. I am Canadian therefore, and Christian in my bones.

Oh, I could move to the United States, renounce my citizenship, start a new life. But I have unrolled a sleeping bag on the Canadian Shield, and felt the rock I hadn't noticed earlier digging all night into my hip. The rock is carried in my body's memory.

As are the lakes. I dove, an awkward, heavy child, into clean water and felt graceful for the first time, swimming. As if I had come home at last. I belong to that water forever.

So I am also Protestant and Christian. Oh, I could renounce the church. I could say it is too timid, while children are hungry; too filled with institutional angst; too filled with uncertain, troubled people like myself.

But I have sat too many Sunday mornings in church and felt the tears come as my soul was touched. I have been loved. I have seen God in a wailing baby lifted for baptism, at a wedding, in a congregation of reluctant mourners when their friend has died.

This identity flows through my veins and cannot be transfused away.

October 31: **Masks**

None of us is able to approach the world without some masks or roles. Consider patient and doctor. If the latter isn't completely garbed in her or his role as doctor, a thorough check-up would be experienced as an unwarranted invasion of the body.

Or reporter. I generally leave to go on assignment a little harassed from getting ready, wondering why anyone would ever trust me with their story. But as soon as I get on the plane something happens. "Mother" and "wife" fall away and I become a reporter, confident, mostly focussed, competent to take your photo and understand what you say.

Problems only arise when the "reporter" (or the doctor or the minister or the politician) think that is all they are, when the mask inflates itself and thinks it has become the whole person. For me, it means I start interviewing people at parties.

No role, no matter how much the world approves, can ever encompass the whole human being.

NOVEMBER

November 1: **Children's art**

Every fridge needs children's art on it. That's because it's art. It's unique. Adults can't do it. And it's given to us: art solely for the sake of art. Children seldom ask payment for their efforts.

Children's art makes a quiet statement of its own about the owner of the fridge. It says that this person respects the young ones. She has the kind of spirituality that honors the most vulnerable. She loves the honesty children bring. And she understands that the most vulnerable part of ourselves is valuable and worthy of protection.

The fridge that is adorned with children's art has a wise owner who knows when the soul has been encountered – in her own self, or in another grownup, or in a child.

We are known by what we treasure.

November 2: **Baking Bread**

The most spiritual thing I do is bake bread. I mix yeast with water, and watch it begin to work. What looked dead is alive. Perhaps that's the little miracle that touches me; I don't know. Then I add flour, and knead for a long time.

While I am kneading I am connected to my grandmother. She baked bread. This old large white bowl was hers.

And I am connected to the field where this flour grew as grain. Never mind about herbicides; I know all about that and I choose to ignore it, choose to believe this flour comes from a farmer who let the wild oats grow up through the grain.

I feel my shoulder muscles work, delight in the strength of my hands, delight in feeding people. No wonder Jesus took this symbol for himself. And before him, it belonged to Demeter, the Goddess of the Harvest, the Grain-mother.

I remember these things, in my small, 20th-century kitchen, pushing my hands into the thick, smooth dough. Old stories flow through me, connecting me to a pair of disciples, shocked into recognition when they break bread with the risen Christ; and to the joyous greening of the earth, the rising of the grain when Demeter's lost daughter, Persephone, returns.

I am kneaded into wholeness, baking bread.

November 3: **Intuition**

We've come to trust our ways of knowing more, women's ways. There's a little tilt lately which favors intuition as much as reason. And we're less inclined to trust the experts, more willing to see what our own innards tell us.

This ought to earn us more respect. It's intuition, after all, that tells us why the baby is crying. And as the child grows, it's subtle hunches that lead us through the jungles of mothering. Oh, slashing away with rules and logic, sharp as a machete, will get us through. But it's easier to follow the old animal trails, lightly, without force.

We should listen to our hunches. It's an old skill, but it serves us well.

November 4: **Work**

When life is out of balance, a dream will come along and say so. When I am working too hard, my mother will appear in a dream, unable to walk and having to pay bills.

The dream is declaring its bias. Whatever it is I am doing, "the mother" part of me is having to pay and is immobilized because of it. I try to pay more attention to the family.

Sometimes the dream will weigh in on the side of the work. Once I dreamed my daughter (she often symbolizes the creative principle) was pulling a baby (my current project) in a wagon. She was wearing roller blades and couldn't stop. (True. If I stopped, it wouldn't get done.) She bumped over a ditch, grabbed a telephone pole, and finally ended up with the baby tossed out of the wagon, but safe. She had made it home, with a lovely healthy child.

I took that healthy child as a statement of faith in the project I was working on at the time, and just kept rolling along.

It's hard to balance our work and the rest of our lives. But we are not alone; millions of other women are wearing the same crazy roller blades.

November 5: **The past**

Signs of my mother aging. She's 83. Almost anything can suddenly send her into a story from the past – how I fell off my tricycle when I was three, the story of my birth, my first date, whatever.

It is incredibly embarrassing.

I have heard of this phenomenon, and I thought it was simply that as short-term memory fades, the elderly are more comfortable living where their memory is sharp. But I think it is more than that. When we, and before us our mothers, grow old, we need to tell the story we carry in our hearts. The story of the family. This wisdom we have gathered, hard-won in diapers and cooking pots, this inheritance, begs to be told.

We need to attend gracefully to the past. It is our future as well.

November 6: **Change**

Should we try to change the world or is it sufficient to change our own selves? It's an important question. Many people spend a great deal of money on analysis, trying to heal themselves. Many people try to change the world, burn out, and have to then spend a great deal of money on therapy.

But some people manage to give themselves away and there is always more. They tangle with tough systems and emerge still human. They never burn out, they just light up everything around them.

I don't know why this is so, but I suspect such people love themselves enough to rest so they can go on. The woman who has learned to love her own self will be gentle with herself, and rest when she needs it.

November 7: **Autonomy**

It's a terrible struggle to grow up and become autonomous, able to provide one's own food and shelter and small pleasures. It is therefore frightening to be intimate. Needing another. Vulnerability goes with the territory of love.

When we take down the walls needed to be our own person, in order to be close to someone else, we lose autonomy.

So we do a little dance: this day close, the next day apart. The steps can be intricate, and even painful when the rhythm doesn't match. Study, dream, meditate, ponder. When we know who we are, we can be close to someone else.

November 8: **Death**

My father died late on the same day he had finished putting the garden to bed for the winter. It was in November. The parsnips had received their requisite touch of frost; he dug them and stored them in the cold cellar. He cleaned the last tools, put them away, and closed up the little storage shed where they would stay all winter.

All was tidy.

I believe this was grace for him. In the spring, tulips would bloom, and then the peonies, the iris, the evening primroses, the day lilies, the daisies, each perennial in its proper order, even without his direction.

I need no further proof of resurrection.

November 9: **Guilt**

I had a student once who suffered from paranoid schizophrenia. The class, though unaware of the nature of his difficulties, waited patiently on him. We knew we were all flawed people.

After the course was over, he would call me. He couldn't sleep, couldn't write, couldn't finish a project he had taken on. I would talk and listen, listen and talk, until he calmed down. It took about an hour. After a couple of years, during an especially busy time, I was slower answering his calls. He drifted away.

I am not proud of this. I am, in fact, filled with shame. He is the age of my sons, and I would wish had this horrible illness struck them, that someone would listen to them when the paralysis of fear entered their hearts.

Sometimes we fail to mother the lost ones who come to us. One reason to believe in God is so that we can believe in forgiveness. We are all flawed people.

November 10: **Faith**

I am always caught in an awkward position around the matter of religion. Going to church is not terrifically popular right now, and I can see why. I crave the stillness of Sunday morning for myself.

But there's something that happens there, in that building, that I can't find in any other place. People sing together. They pray together, treating the universe as if it is alive and can hear them. They hear the story quietly. They don't try on Sunday morning to decide if it is true or not (that's saved for Bible study during the week); they just receive it.

They are gentle with one another, mostly; even if they are having a fight, there is a truce just on that one day. And most of all, if they listen hard, they will hear this strange injunction to love one another and above all the poor; a piece of advice which would be laughed out of any corporate boardroom.

Re-ligion means re-connection. Perhaps religion – awkwardly, it's practiced by humans, after all – reconnects us with some past wisdom we have set aside. Inside those walls we willingly suspend the modern age, and let the past, and perhaps the future, speak.

November 11: **Immortality**

My 83-year-old mother can't write down her dreams, because she is blind. Instead she phones immediately the next morning and tells them to me.

Not long ago, she described one in which a friend who died recently and my father and her mother and other relatives (all of whom died years ago) stood on the bank of a river, beckoning her to cross on a plank.

"No-o-o-o," she said in the dream.

"I didn't know if I could make it across," she confided to me afterward.

I was shaken by the invitation of the dream, at the same time as I was relieved that she wasn't ready to accept it.

"What did it feel like?" I said, when I could speak.

"Oh, it felt wonderful," she said. "That place across the river – it was full of light. And I could see."

No matter what the body does, the soul knows it will live forever.

November 12: **Boredom**

My 17-year-old daughter has taken to coming into my office and flinging herself on the couch. "I'm bored," she announces. The dog, sensing disquiet, hovers, looking as if he might take up the same cry.

She hasn't been bored since she was six, just before she began school.

It's a good sign. We are only bored when we are ready to move into a new stage. For her, it's time to leave home and be treated as an adult (which her teachers can't quite do, having known her since she was a shy 13-year-old.)

Boredom is not confined to teenagers. It marks every life passage, pushing us to leave an outgrown mental or emotional framework. It wants to be carefully noted and questioned: where is it pushing us to go?

November 13: **Nightmares**

Scary dreams, for all their reputation, only ask one thing. Our attention. Write them down. We can turn to the most fearsome player in the dream – the dragon, the flood, the raging storm – and say, "Why are you in my dream?"

When it answers, write that down too.

It will give you something to pray over.

The next night, if the dream comes back (invited by your interest, they often do) you will find the dragon or the storm less fierce, and more conversational.

It could be the beginning of a fruitful relationship.

November 14: **Rituals**

In a cold November wind, my mother-in-law's ashes, in a tiny container, were gently placed in the ground. Prayers were said. It was the last in a series of loving rituals celebrated by a large family, to honor the woman who had raised them well.

Now it is stamped on our hearts. We, her children and the ones who married her children, are the oldest now. We are the ones called to be, simultaneously, wiser and a little more frail. It is expected. Our own children, whom once we carried in backpacks and on bicycle seats, will ceremoniously open doors and carry packages for us.

"When I die," I tell my daughter on the way

home, "I would like my ashes carried to the top of Maple Mountain and scattered to the wind."

"What will I do with the container?" she says, not minding the canoe trip to get there, nor the climb, but ever practical.

"Pack it out," I say, alarmed she would have to ask.

"No, no," she says delicately. "Would you put something like that in the recycling bin?"

So, laughing but deadly serious, we negotiate our changing status. She can't grow up completely until I relinquish power. And I do so willingly, handing over my own future ashes to her.

Rituals mark our growth toward wisdom.

November 15: **Community**

Parenting is too hard to do alone, or with a partner. We need to surround ourselves with surrogate mothers, aunts, uncles, friends.

Churches are sometimes good at this. They can, at their best, provide a community of Christmas pageants, junior choirs, and people who know our children's names. There is nothing more wonderful for a child than the sense of being surrounded by aunts and uncles and grandmothers and grandfathers who love them in their wholeness – wriggly, vocal, holy – and who give them a spiritual past.

Our children need to know they are the result of the love of thousands.

November 16: **Bread**

The secret of baking bread is to remember it is alive. It doesn't like to be chilled, and it likes your hands on it. Keep it covered in a warm place, knead it appreciatively, and inspect it every once in awhile as it rises.

Like seedlings and people who are ill, growing yeast responds to loving intentionality and warm thoughts by visibly expanding.

We don't have to think about the oven.

November 17: **Laziness**

I don't know any lazy women. I'm sure there must be some somewhere. But the women I know don't suffer from sloth.

The balance we require is more along the lines of getting our heads up long enough to see what some (often men) call the overview. We are usually so immersed in the details (is that paper in my briefcase, what's for dinner, who's picking up the children from gymnastics) it's hard to think of the big picture.

A certain amount of what looks a lot like laziness – sitting, ambling, gazing into space – is needed to discover the Meaning of Life.

November 18: **Self-consciousness**

Grownups are prone to describing some children as being "terribly self-conscious" or "shy." They're the ones who can't stand up in class without blushing.

Now that I'm a grownup myself, I have another view of self-consciousness. It's not unrelated to that of the young ones. Their ability to stand outside themselves and observe what their own self is doing almost incapacitates them; but – in a less-lethal form – it's exactly what we need to raise children and to do other crucial tasks.

We need to be able to stand outside our self and observe our conversations with our children, or our boss, or our employees, or our husband. We need to see what's happening, hear how we sound. We need to wonder (later, in recollection, will do) if this remark was provoked by a memory of childhood pain, or that one by the clash of contrasting personality types.

At best, self-awareness prevents damage to relationships, especially with children. At worst, it can only make us blush.

November 19: **Children**

Our friend, who is five, was sitting in church waiting for his family's turn to go downstairs for the yearly turkey supper, a highly-organized and much-loved annual event.

A family acquaintance, also waiting, came over to say hello, and offered a handshake. Our friend paused, wondering what to do. Then he reached out and shook the offered hand seriously, looking up out of blue five-year-old eyes. "The peace of Christ be with you," he said.

Indeed. It is.

November 20: **Writing**

Journalism is a dangerous occupation. It involves loosening the boundaries between you and your subject, opening yourself up to feel their emotion and know their truths.

Sometimes those operative emotions are grief, anger, confusion. Once I spent an afternoon sitting on the grass with a man who had watched while his peoples' land, their spiritual mother, had been carved – by government action or lassitude – over the years into smaller and smaller pieces. A chunk of their mother for a seaway here, a highway there, a golf course. Now an army surrounded them. His gentle younger brother was on a barricade. He told the story, sometimes weeping. I sat dazed by his pain.

This must be done. It's especially important for those who try to read and write by the light of the gospel. If writers don't allow themselves to risk their hearts being captured by the people they observe, they will report only from the vantage point of the status quo. And God hardly ever lives there.

November 21: **Writing**

Journalists enter a place and let it enter their own hearts in return. At least, that's what I do. I hear many stories, especially from those who think they have no story to tell. And once I have allowed the skin to be peeled away from my heart, then I stand back.

I put the boundaries between myself and others in place again in order to write. I allow a kind of distance to settle on me. I work, as a writer, from a strange place of remembered emotion – feeling, evoked from many questions, and distilled through the history of the place and the voices of people of opposing visions, and finally, through my own experience.

In this peculiar place, I hope for truth.

People imagine journalists are brave. Perhaps some are. But the bravest thing they ever do is dare to tell another person's story.

November 22: **Education**

Sometimes women get locked into a certain way of thinking about themselves. We shouldn't do that, we have too much to lose. Some of us might think – for example – we can't approach God, or talk about God, because we don't have enough education in theology.

It's wonderful to be well-educated in theology. But sometimes a good theological education only has to be unlearned. God turns out to be a woman, as well as a man, after all those years with a beard. "Blessed are the poor" turns out to mean precisely that, after all our years of adding "...in spirit" to make those of us who aren't, feel better. Someone notices there are two versions of the origin of the sexes in Genesis, and maybe God didn't make the original woman out of Adam's rib after all.

A little learning is a dangerous thing.

November 23: **Growing Older**

In some cultures, women of a certain age are allowed to make lewd remarks and explicit jokes without censure. Their lack of status as sexual creatures allows them a freedom from cultural restraints younger women don't enjoy.

I haven't felt compelled to be any more lewd than usual. But when I turned 40, a voice I had never encountered before began whispering in my head whenever anyone phoned to ask me to volunteer for this or that. "I'm 40 years old and I can do what I like," the voice said. And I began to say no to doing what I didn't really wish to do.

When I turned 50, the voice got louder. I don't think I became terminally selfish, but now I ask that whatever I do have meaning for me, that it not rise out of anyone else's expectations.

In many cultures, one gift that comes with middle age is freedom.

November 24: **Gifts**

One fast way to burn out is not to use our particular gifts.

Often we don't name them because we are inclined to dwell on our limitations instead. But it's a good idea to figure out what those gifts are. Then we can stop wondering what we are supposed to do with our lives. Dithering takes more energy than doing something with passion.

Some have compassion; to encounter such a woman is to be heard at the deepest level, and strengthened.

Some have courage; to encounter such a woman is to be challenged and encouraged to think.

Some have a gift for discernment. They help the rest of us find our way, if we ask.

Spiritual disciplines – prayer, walking, dreaming, meditating – help us find the gift we have.

November 25: **Communities**

People will always disappoint us. Since we and they are not gods, they can do nothing else. Even the gods, for that matter, fell far short of perfect behavior. This is true of people in spiritual communities, too, whether they are churches or small groups that meet just to talk or to work together.

So if our spiritual communities prove to be intractable and cranky, argumentative and confused, we might try just relaxing. They are human.

November 26: **Walking**

Just a few days ago, a friend and I went down by the water to walk. We hadn't seen each other for a week or so and we were used to visiting more often.

It was warm for November. We found ourselves on a narrow path, looking for dried grasses and sumac branches to take home. We found rose bushes covered with rose hips and, delighted, we broke them off, gathering branches until our arms were full.

This is the way of women's friendships: walking and talking, and sharing pleasure in beauty, sharing worries and small joys.

We brought our bundles home, unwieldy by now, and said goodbye.

She reappeared a few days later with another armload of the rose-hipped branches. I filled a basket on the porch.

The next day it snowed, sifting over the rich red berries on my front porch.

I see my friend whenever I look at it, see the last afternoon of autumn, the last day of warmth by the open lake before the winter. And I am happy.

November 27: **Travel**

In the African Church of the Holy Spirit, people pray before travel from one village to another, that they will be kept safe, and again, when they come home, that God will hear their thanks.

They take off their shoes when they pray because they stand on holy ground.

How much more we who travel daily on vast highways at high speeds need to pray.

November 28: **Cathedrals**

The great stone cathedrals and the serene country churches of Germany all have great high pulpits, so the people must look up and be properly respectful of the preachers' words. The churches are filled with paintings and sculpture and music that flows like water on a hot day.

How is it that these soaring structures, for all their attentiveness to faith and for all their loveliness, could not contain the ugliness that burst forth in the Holocaust? How could evil be so strong?

There is no answer to this.

If evil could be contained in an answer, it would not exist. But it does. All we can do is add our love, bit by bit, to the mix, in the hope of creating a critical mass that will be enough to keep it at bay.

November 29: **Spiritual discipline/ walking**

Spiritual discipline is a strange term, conjuring up a Gothic atmosphere of bleak rooms and cold churches. It's all we have, though, to describe our deliberate efforts to be close to God.

The spiritual discipline I would choose would be to dance; but while God would no doubt be touched by my awkward efforts, I would not. Instead, all winter, I walk.

Out the front door, down the long side street and past Mr. Sweetman's garden piled high with snow and waiting for spring, over the railway tracks and across busy Main Street, over more tracks, and suddenly I am assaulted by light and space and winter-brown weedstalks lifting through the snow. I walk out on the frozen lake and turn to see my whole, lovely, tattered northern city stretched before me.

My soul expands. I am made joyful by walking on water. So it must have been for Jesus, pacing across the sea of Galilee, turning to look in awe at what God and God's busy creatures had made.

A spiritual discipline is whatever helps us see through the eyes of God.

November 30: **Men**

There's some merit in hanging out at parties with the men. We can learn so much from the way they appear, at least, to be. They seem comfortable in their bodies, not worrying if they are too thin or too thick or not muscular enough. They seem self-confident, sure that people will still love them even if they don't take on more than they can handle.

It's always wise to develop aspects within us we don't know very well, and those are often mirrored in men.

DECEMBER

December 1: **Angels**

Nothing convinces me more that this materialistic age has a powerful spiritual shadow than the stories I hear about angels. Somewhere in our unconscious, unknown to us, but constantly breaking through in ways we can't control, is a yearning for connection with God.

By the world's standard, these stories have no logic. By the internal reasoning of the soul, they make perfect sense.

A lawyer (they're trained in rules, impeccably skeptical) told me a story about his friend, a

Jehovah's Witness and therefore required to do many hours of "witnessing" door-to-door per month. Normally this work is done in pairs. But she was behind in her requirements and set out alone. She rang the doorbell at one house where the occupant, a large man, seemed agitated; she spoke to him, but left in short order.

Later, her testimony helped place him at home at the time she had called, where he had just murdered his wife.

He hadn't hurt the young woman (a witness in more ways than one) he said, because of the big guy who was with her.

December 2: **Friends**

One of the loveliest ways to friendship is shared creation. No wonder husbands and wives are sometimes such good friends. They create so many things together.

And women become friends starting a nursery school, lobbying a school board, sharing a study group, bringing different foods for a pot luck supper, talking as they watch their mutual vision take shape. Singing in the choir, making a lovely sound. Together.

Oh there's walking together, too, lingering over coffee, gossiping. It's all part of friendship. But a friendship built on a shared office, or a shared goal, or on each other's children – talking through their worries, creating grown-up humans – *that* is a friendship infinitely strong, tempered by the task before it.

December 3: **Ordinary Gods**

My life as a woman is busier than my mother's was. Oh, she did mountains of ironing (I don't), cleaned the house until it shone (ours doesn't), and served nutritious meals (I don't want to think about that.)

I don't do any of those things because I'm spending my time glued to a computer, as are many of my women friends. We have marched into the wage economy with a vengeance, and our lives are stretched, especially if we have small children.

How can we possibly have time for God?

Enter the Celtic tradition. Its adherents had a faith which offers us much, one in which God is all around and with us in the every-day, the only days we women have. From the lighting of the peat fire in the morning to the cold water splashed from a pitcher on their face and hands, to the milking of cows and sleeping again, their whole day was lived in the light of God.

We have no peat fires. But we are alike in having little time for long periods of meditation or esoteric spiritual disciplines.

We could rediscover their sense of God around us. If it's hard to say a prayer in front of a computer, we could turn away and look out the window. We could pray in traffic; and at dinner. And at bedtime, no matter how tired.

The Creator surrounds and blesses all Her creatures, especially when we are exhausted.

December 4: **Making beds**

An old Celtic prayer finds God even in the midst

of making the bed. That small ordinary task becomes filled with radiance:

I make this bed
In the name of the Father, the Son and the Holy Ghost,
In the name of the night we were conceived,
In the name of the night that we were born,
In the name of the day we were baptized,
In the name of each night, each day,
Each angel that is in the heavens. *

Maybe it is harder to receive that sense of all the angels in heaven surrounding us when we are turning on the computer in the morning; their lustrous drift of wings and music seems at odds with resolutely logical tools. But cooking supper, walking, bathing children, tucking them into bed...

The past still comes to meet us; and life still moves one day, one night, one angel at a time.

* Douglas Hyde: *Religious Songs of Connacht*, London, Dublin, 1906, II republished with an introduction by Dominic Daly, Irish University Press, Shannon, Ireland, 1972 p. 207

December 5: **Something now**

I overheard our two sons, David and Andy, talking when they were five and three respectively. Both were equipped with paint and paper. They were happily swirling the one on the other, and on their father's old shirts worn as smocks.

"What's it going to be, Andy?" asked David, in his best kind-big-brother fashion.

"It's something now," said Andy happily, as he continued painting.

Our lives are not waiting to happen. We are something now.

December 6: **Women's medicine**

Ojibway elder Art Solomon tells a story about the healing of the earth. When I am afraid, I think of this and feel hope.

Solomon feels strongly that we need to hear the voice of women. In the beginning there was harmony, but the world is now out of balance, missing too much of the feminine principle. "Women have to pick up their medicine to heal a troubled world," he says.

He was challenged on that by a young woman, who wanted to know what women's medicine was. He thought about that over the winter and finally came up with the answer.

"I came to the conclusion," he said with care, "that women *are* the medicine."

December 7: **Seeking God**

Looking for God is like writing a poem; in fact it may be precisely the same thing. Demanding that a poem or a glimpse of God be given to us doesn't work; we can only put ourselves in the way of both, and hope we have sufficient strength to cope when they arrive.

In fact, the art of looking for God may be simply building up strength: singing, praying, learning the nuances of God's language, finding companions in the search.

Then, when it is revealed that God is homeless, we will have a church (the house of God, after all) waiting so She can come in from the cold. And we will have the strength to challenge public policy for Her.

December 8: **Angels**

Angels. From the Greek *angelos,* messenger from God. In the Christian tradition, believers are admonished to welcome strangers into their homes, because they may be "angels unaware."

Exactly who the "unaware" one is in the passage is a little ambiguous, though. Is it the potential host? Or are the angels, themselves, unaware they are angels?

Our oldest son, coming up to his 15th birthday, wanted no party; he just wanted his grandparents to come for dinner.

Delighted, my parents decided they would make the two-hour journey by train. In his concern to catch the train, my father didn't realize until he reached the station that he had forgotten his heart pills. The train had already pulled in.

But the conductor knew him well; they had worked together. He knew my parents lived a five-minute drive away. "I'll hold the train," he said,"You get what you need."

So the train waited and Grandpa made it to his grandson's birthday party, Grandpa's infectious chuckle running like a bright thread through the whole day.

Two days later, back home, he was dead. The heart that needed those pills had suffered one final assault. We were left with a multitude of memories, none more cherished than a last party that only happened because one railway employee made a train five minutes late.

An angel might wear a conductor's uniform "without knowing it." Or flour-dusted jeans, or a shirt with baby's spit on it.

December 9: **Darkness**

This month of short days and long nights is a fine month for looking inward. Part of the cycle of human existence is going into the darkness, into the earth. Persephone disappearing below, going down to Hades while her mother keens above and turns the earth to winter.

We need these times when we descend into our own shadow, our own forgotten, wounded selves. Such times demand we pull out a notebook, imagine, write to these lost parts of us, talk to them, heal them.

After that, we will be stronger. Persephone returned to earth wiser, matured – a woman. If we allow our darknesses to teach us, we, like her, will rise stronger than before.

December 10: **Guilt**

It is not possible to do and be everything our children want us to do and be. Nor is it possible to do and be everything our spouses, lovers, or parents want us to be. We can be gentle with ourselves on that basis. We can only be what we are.

December 11: **Greed**

I confess. I walk into the linen department of any large store and I look at those soft, thick towels in those heavenly colors and I want them all. More than I can ever use. I want to pile them up in a linen closet, stuff them into trunks, layer the bathroom and count them. I am like Midas with his gold.

For some of us, it's shoes. Or houses, or gold jewelry, or food.

Mostly, spiritual teachings suggest we live simply. And that's very wise, because true greed feeds on itself and grows bigger and wants more. But on the way to living simply, we need to be gentle with the hungry child within. (That's where the greed comes from. All that yearning for gold or chocolate cake comes from a tiny voice inside saying "I want, I'm starved. Feeeeed me...")

" I know," you can murmur. "I know. And I love you. It's all right."

It's never too late to be a well-loved child.

December 12: **Compensation**

Our dreams can be counted on to note imbalance in our lives, and to try to tilt us back to health. If we are extremely solitary, they will nudge us toward people. If we are overly work-oriented, they will push us in another direction. Once I had a dream of my dog, Gabriel, leaping and dancing in a sunny field of wildflowers, careless and free, doing nothing more important than a whimsical Snoopy dance.

That was the whole dream. It went on and on, my spirit nudging me to let my animal nature (my body) dance. Not for nothing is our dog named Gabriel, the announcing angel, the bringer of good news. If there is no resonance between our dream-actions and our waking life, no similarity of any kind, a dream may be simply trying to balance our life for us.

But why should dreams have all the fun?

December 13: **Absence**

At Christmas there are those who are profoundly present by their absence. Especially that first Christmas when – without thought – their name goes on your shopping list. Then you remember.

Some deaths, those who died too young, create a void so huge it changes our lives forever and blasts a hole in any holiday or any day at all.

But these others, these logical deaths of those whose time had rightly come, these we still remember with love and memory and joy mingled with regret. They fill our Christmas fabric with small holes, like lace, letting in light and memories.

Christmas is never a holiday of entirely unabashed delight; remembered laughter always echoes just behind the present. The perfect, happy, innocent Christmas we strive for can't be done. We might want to try for a real one.

December 14: **Workaholism**

It's trendy right now to talk of one's workaholism. There's a certain cachet to this addiction, especially for women. There's something about losing your soul to a computer that seems more respectable than ambling down Main St. begging loonies for a bottle.

I have difficulty, though, with this prevailing paradigm – everyone addicted, trapped, sick, everyone the victim of external forces they are struggling to overcome. It trivializes the chronic pain in which many live.

Still, it can be helpful. As with any addiction, work is always in danger of separating me from my friends, my spouse, my body. And viewing as an illness my ability to flee into work when I am faced with something distasteful, like conflict, holds up the possibility of healing.

Death will be the only cure. I love my work too much to have any illusions about that. But healing – learning to live with it, learning to carry on relationships and find meaning in life and live in community at the same time – now *that* is possible.

Workaholism, like any chronic illness, may not be curable. But we *can* be healed.

December 15: **Rituals**

Rituals assume a life of their own. Many years ago, I lived in a northern mining town where everything in the grocery store was stale, having arrived by boxcar anytime during the week. One of the long-timers took me to her home for a day and taught me, in her soft Newfoundland accent, how to make bread.

I began to make tea rings at Christmas, fabulous concoctions of fresh bread laden with nuts and cinnamon and raisins. "Couldn't we give one to..." my husband would wheedle. Proud of my baking, I made more and more.

Such arrogance returns to haunt me. For the whole month of December, now, the kitchen smells of rising bread and cinnamon. The first Christmas away from home, for the oldest children, is marked by a request for the recipe; and those remaining have learned, offhandedly, on their way through the kitchen, to roll out dough, slap on butter, add sugar and cinnamon.

This doesn't make me cranky, as repetitive tasks normally do. This floury kitchen and the sweet-smelling mounds of dough are at odds with the rest of my life; but they are traditions in a life that is carried on by quickly-written and soon-erased e-mail. This bread, this ritual, connects me with another life, when a gentle older woman taught a young woman to make bread when we were far from bakeries, and home.

December 16: **Christmas tea rings**

Make a batch of any yeast-risen sweet roll dough. You can double the recipe. (The recipe I use, doubled, requires about 14 cups of flour.) After it has risen twice, divide it into four pieces.

Roll out each piece into an oblong; spread it with butter, then sprinkle with brown sugar (about 1/2 cup for an oblong about 15 x 9"). Sprinkle generously with cinnamon, then with 1/2 cup raisins. Roll up tightly, beginning at the wide side, and seal the edge by pinching it together. Place sealed-edge down in a ring on a lightly greased baking sheet. Pinch ends together to make a circle.

With scissors, make cuts 2/3 of the way through the ring, at 1" intervals. Turn each of these sections on their side. (Be firm, bread dough can take it.) Let rise until double. Bake at 375°F for 25 to 30 minutes. (Check to make sure it doesn't get too brown.) While still warm, frost with a simple white icing and decorate with nuts and cherries. Serve warm. (You can wrap in foil and freeze, and reheat later in the same foil.)

December 17: **Gabriel**

The angel Gabriel is one of the four angels who surround the throne of God. He is the one who appears to Mary, and tells her not to be afraid, that she is blessed among women. He is the bringer of good news, in charge of the moon and the month of January and the direction North on the compass. And he is made of fire.

None of this is important, really. Except that if you frequent churches at all, and if you happen to attend a Christmas pageant, it's likely you will see him. He'll be about ten, wearing a sheet and cardboard wings and looking sheepish. "Peace be with you," he will say. He will then make a long speech to Mary about the son who is to be born to her, concluding with these words: "For there is nothing that God cannot do."

For this reassurance, we need to welcome Gabriel when he appears.

December 18: **Exhaustion**

Something happens at Christmas to set every

perfectionist bone in our bodies aching. It's the magazines, maybe, with all that glitter. Or it's childhood. Either our mothers produced a magnificent Christmas and we need to do the same, or – covered in the gloss of memory – we think they did.

Some women genuinely love the season, and by their joy in decorating and baking cookies, and gorgeously wrapping gifts, and stringing lights and writing big long personal cards to everyone they know set the rest of us into a fierce spiral of competition.

Some women need the season to be fiercely busy, to hide the fact that someone is missing.

Some women, conscientious types, make Christmas a tornado of achievement (so many parties given this year, so many cards addressed and mailed) like everything else in their lives.

Perhaps this season is simply a heightened version of how we are in everyday life. Something new wants to be born in us, though – maybe rest, joy, tenderness. That's what Christmas is about. Something new being born.

December 19: **Christmas**

Young children can be wounded by excess at Christmas. And there is a sweet irony in the birth of a poor peasant Jew being marked by the exchange of expensive gifts and the creaking of so many overloaded credit cards.

But if the engine of the economy must be stimulated by some event, reasons a friend, what better than the celebration of Jesus' birth? Mmm, I think. That would be fine, if only all children, rich and poor, would be so blessed with toys.

Still. We forget that – for Christians – the real high holiday is Easter, when Jesus rose from the dead.

Perhaps at Christmas we should accept the Dionysian quality that keeps breaking through – the food and drink and feasting and gifts and parties. It gets us through the darkness of December. Perhaps the pagan gods, to whom this solstice once belonged, should be honored also. Perhaps Christmas is a time to find a way to be foolish and extravagant with all children, rich and poor.

December 20: **Christmas gifts**

The real joy of Christmas gifts is the opportunity they offer to write "love,..." on the card. Most of us hardly ever tell our friends we love them, even when it's true. It's not a habit of our culture.

December 21: **Holidays**

Our lives are measured by the holy days of faith. How could the year have any shape at all without Christmas as a vantage point? Or Easter, year by year the presence of the resurrection announced with lilies and alleluias.

The confusion found in some public schools around religious holidays is surprising; especially in those whose administrators declare, with excellent intentions, that children can't sing Christmas carols. As if our children didn't need meaning, an astonishing misapprehension on the part of those supposed to be educators.

Religious observance in public schools is important. Chanukah, Diwali, Passover, Winter Solstice, Wesak, Ram Navani all offer a chance to ponder mystery. Children can easily see that God appears in many different ways. This knowledge holds none of the terror for children that it does for adults.

December 22: **Heaven**

One Christmas, four friends, a family, came to visit from Japan. They had never been to Canada. We saw our home, the frozen lake, the trails in the bush through their eyes. Our small northern city became enchanted, an other-worldly place of impossible temperatures and a cold white moon that climbed into the sky and lit the universe. One night they stayed up to watch it moving through the trees. They snuggled down on the living room rug in front of the fireplace. The dignified father of the family had kept a fire blazing all week, adding wood and playing with the coals the way our children had always played, delighted, with the fire at camp.

Again I learned that this is heaven. Now. Here. This ordinary human house, chilly in winter. This familiar mortal city, with its trains and school buses and corner stores curling around the edge of an ancient lake. This not-perfect but created community, of not-perfect but much-loved creatures of God. We who live on earth also live in heaven now, and it is our sorrow if we are so busy we fail to notice.

December 23: **Christmas dinner**

Shopping, peeling, organizing. It's getting close to the day. For Christmas dinner there will be *latkes*, made by our friend Rose – potato pancakes with applesauce, to go with the turkey and stuffing.

We celebrate Chanukah together and birthdays and graduations and events of all kinds. My daughter has several mothers – including Rose, who is among other things, single, resilient, bright, and strong. My daughter learns that there are many ways of being woman.

It takes a whole village to raise a child.

December 24: **Hope**

At 11 o'clock on Christmas Eve, the church is full. Many are people unknown to one another, people who attend rarely. There are familiar readings, a simple message, communion. Unlit candles are handed out with the bread and wine.

And always, the same ending. The lights go out. There is a little silence, and then this congregation of strangers begins to sing, "Silent night, Holy night..." into the soft darkness. Even the most unchurched know the words. A single candle is carried down the aisle, its flame passing along each row, candle by candle; and the church fills with a gentle illumination we see only once a year, a clear yellow light from the meeting of darkness and fire.

It is impossible – this place, these people, this light, this yearning for a better world, inexpressible except in song and flame. The impossible is made possible by hope.

Silent night. Holy night. Sleep in heavenly peace.

December 25: **Christmas Day**

Perhaps we have been consumed with wrapping and gifts and food and whether or not everyone will find what they wanted under the tree. Maybe there is guilt; we can't afford what we wanted to give. Perhaps there is hurry; a sumptuous feast to organize, will the turkey be cooked, will everyone fit around the table...

Stop.

It's all right. These things are part of this remarkable day, so crammed with memory it can scarcely bear it, with guilt and pleasure and laughter and mourning all mixed up with and created by our childhood.

It's all right. This is the day God comes to bring God's promised reign. This is the Shalom when the lion and the lamb, the hungry and the weak, lie down peacefully together. And we who have wrapped the presents and cared for those who have been given to us as friends or family or both, that peace comes to us as to everyone.

If the baby, the child-born-in-a-manger, lives – and I believe with all my heart he does – he lives in all of us. He lives in our souls and our hearts and our arms, weary, perhaps, from preparing for his coming. We are the manger, the stable, the shepherds, the kings, the joyful angels. We are Mary, the blessed one of God. We are the Shalom.

December 26: **Music**

I have a friend who heard music when she was a child, out in a field alone. She came home and told her mother she had heard angels singing. No one, as far as her mother knew, had ever talked to her of angels. She hadn't studied them in Sunday school. She was only a little girl.

She believes in angels still.

Music comes from God so directly to all people. It must be our soul's memory of another life that makes it so familiar to us.

December 27: **Tradition**

Tradition can be a great weight for women. Probably we should examine long-held traditions each Christmas, to see if there any that have become too heavy and deserve to be retired.

But tradition is also something women love, something that frames our lives with meaning. The tree in the same place each Christmas, the cookies and milk set out for Santa as long as the kids believe, because that is what our parents did with us. The passing on of these small actions to the next generation, later.

Traditions give us comfort.

December 28: **What if?**

What if Toronto's buildings had been more influenced by Douglas Cardinal than Le Corbusier? What if more buildings, in all our cities, were flowing and organic instead of needles pointing to the sky? What if our world-view had more love of the earth in it, and less of the need to rise above it?

December 29: **Senex**

A thought for the end of the year, after reading James Hillman's description of senex energy, the wisdom of the old. Any era, he says, is always dominated by a certain collection of the energies we carry within ourselves. If it becomes too one-sided, one aspect too completely in control, this is not good. No matter what the energy is, if it is one-sided – allowed to go to its extreme – it is dangerous.

By his description, we could say ours is a senex culture, a culture of old men fascinated by economics, the concrete, numbers, figures. A culture without soul.

Not a good culture for women. Not because we have a unique claim on matters of the soul, or because we don't like math, but because much of what concerns us can't be defined by economics. Children and how they will be fed and how they will be safe; the very old and how they will be cared for.

We cannot forget the soul, nor destroy the energy of the young.

December 30: **Ambiguity**

In dream work, the dreamer is often asked to turn the events in the dream upside down. If there is a death in the dream, we ask, "Is there something in me that needs to die?" If someone is attacked by a vicious animal with a terrible grip, we ask "Is there a situation in my life where tenacity is required?"

This only reflects the need to live with uncertainty and grey areas in much of our lives. Sometimes an action we feel we must take is only the lesser of two evils. Sometimes the truth is hard to find and seems to shift from day to day.

Many of us are uncomfortable with such ambiguity. We are tempted to run to a safe place, any place that's certain and sure, just to escape the pain of not really knowing. Some of us fit into the personality type that likes precision, decisions made, options tidied up.

But it's best not to shut down our wondering and pondering too soon. The certainty we jump to may be dogmatic or unthinking or wrong.

December 31: **Grace Note**

I've always liked the image of myself as an unflappable hostess. But once, the night before a large New Year's Day Brunch (hosted by our family) a too-riotous New Year's Eve party (hosted by our middle child) resulted in mess, confusion, and a sleepless night. I was furious.

The son in question was penitent. We were all exhausted. An hour before the brunch we were solemnly cleaning up. Not speaking. Finally I began "I love you, but..." He didn't even let me get any further with my buts. "I know, and that's why I feel so bad..."

A minute later we were hugging one another, both sobbing, imminent arrival of guests forgotten while we assured each other of our affection.

The brunch was fine. He grew out of wild New Year's Eve parties, I think that night. And I grew out of inviting too many people for brunch in the middle of the busiest season of the year. I finally figured out how to drop the mask of the hostess and settle for being a mom who loves her kids, young and grown-up.

Index

A

B

C

D

E

F

G

H

I

J

K

L

M

N

O

S